# 天津历史风貌建筑
# HISTORIC ARCHITECTURE IN TIANJIN

## 居住建筑卷一
## Residential Buildings Volume 1

路红 主编

天津大学出版社
TIANJIN UNIVERSITY PRESS

# 《天津历史风貌建筑丛书》编写组
## AUTHORS GROUP


主　　编：路　红
副 主 编：唐连蒙　徐连和　孙　超　关　静
编　　辑：王志青　张俊东　李琦琳　孔　晖　金彭育　陈广发　孙　巍
　　　　　李　莉　谈卫卫　肖　楠　姚　鑫　袁　勇　何效星
摄　　影：何　方　何　易

Editor-in-chief: Lu Hong
Associate Editors: Tang Lianmeng, Xu Lianhe, Sun Chao, Guan Jing
Editors: Wang Zhiqing, Zhang Jundong, Li Qilin, Kong Hui, Jin Pengyu,
Chen Guangfa, Sun Wei, Li Li, Tan Weiwei, Xiao Nan,
Yao Xin, Yuan Yong, He Xiaoxing
Photographers: He Fang, He Yi

# 序

城市是人类文明的结晶。在城市的发展和延续过程中，必然会形成一些文化内涵丰富的历史建筑遗存，留下体现时代特征的文化印痕。天津历史风貌建筑就是记载着天津城市“历史年轮”和发展历程的“史书”。

读到由几本集子构成的“天津历史风貌建筑”系列丛书清样时，我深深地被天津市拥有的数量大、类型多、富有特色的历史风貌建筑吸引、陶醉。徜徉在这些承载着厚重历史的建筑里，会感受到天津城市发展的曲折经历和人民群众的不朽业绩。这批历史风貌建筑有的已成为天津的文化标志，有的则融入了居民的日常生活，是维系天津城市生命和形象的重要细胞。

天津地处大运河的北端，濒临渤海。从春秋战国时代的军事重镇蓟州，到明、清两个封建王朝的京畿门户和连通南北水运的重要枢纽，天津遗存了独乐寺、文庙、天后宫、玉皇阁等风格瑰丽、气势恢宏的中国传统建筑。近代以来，租界内代表东、西方文化特色和交融的各式历史建筑，林林总总，伫立于津沽大地，构成近代天津城市的独特肌理。所有这些，形成了天津与北京、上海等城市风格迥异的城市风貌，是天津城市文化的独特元素和魅力所在。

天津的历史风貌建筑大部分建成于19世纪末和20世纪前半叶，它们集中反映了中国近代以来的风云际会：既有帝国主义列强对我国领土的侵略，又有中国人民不屈的抗争；既有封建社会末期的社会变革，又有辛亥革命以来的中国民主革命的斗争历程；既有西方建筑艺术的特色和风格，更有天津人民的智慧和包容。因此，纵览天津历史建筑和文化遗产，犹如在阅读一部中国近现代建筑的历程。

感谢天津市委、市政府和文物保护、历史风貌建筑保护部门，以及相关专家学者的辛勤努力，于2005年制定了《天津市历史风貌建筑保护条例》，对这些建筑进行了修缮，保护了大批尚未列入各级文物保护单位的历史建筑，使之成为天津历史文化遗产的一个重要组成部分。同时，经过修缮的历史建筑既能够得到有效保护和传承，也惠及了当代百姓，使城市的建筑文化记忆不会中断。

关于天津的历史建筑希望人们能从本书入手，了解它们，触摸它们，感受它们。愿城市历史建筑的保护工作在全国各地蓬勃发展，也愿“天津历史风貌建筑”系列丛书为全国文化遗产保护和研究工作带个好头。

国家文物局局长　单霁翔

2010年4月

# Preface

Cities are the crystallization of human civilization. During the process of urban development, some historical buildings with rich cultural connotations would definitely remain. They are the cultural stamps reflecting the characteristics of the times. Tianjin Historical Buildings are like a "history book" recording the growth rings of Tianjin urban development.

When reading the press proof of volumes of the book series entitled *Historic Architecture in Tianjin*, I was deeply impressed and intoxicated by the historical buildings in Tianjin that are large in number, abundant in types and unique in features. Wandering in these buildings full of historical deposition, you will feel the ups and downs of Tianjin's urban development as well as the achievements made by people. Some of these historical buildings have become the cultural symbols of Tianjin; some have been integrated into people's daily life and become significant to maintain the life and image of Tianjin.

Located at the north end of the Grand Canal and adjoining the Bohai Sea, Tianjin used to be Ji State, an important military town in the Spring and Autumn and the Warring States Periods, and the gate to the capital city as well as an important water transport junction connecting the south to the north in the Ming and Qing Dynasties. Some traditional Chinese buildings still remain in Tianjin including the Dule Temple, the Confucian Temple, the Temple for Queen of Heaven and the Taoist Temple of Jade Emperor, which are all magnificent and gorgeous. Since modern times, a variety of buildings representing the mingling of oriental and western cultures started to stand in the concessions. They gave the city a unique look, and made Tianjin quite different in urban style from Beijing and Shanghai. It also explains why the city culture of Tianjin has a distinctive appeal.

Most of the historical buildings in Tianjin were completed at the end of the nineteenth century and in the first half of the twentieth century. They are telling us the eventful history in modern China, including the invasion of our territories by imperialist powers and the unyielding resistance of Chinese people, the social reforms happened at the end of the feudal society and the journey of the democratic revolution since the Revolution of 1911, the features and styles of western architecture and the wisdom and the all-embracing tolerance of Tianjin people. Therefore, viewing Tianjin historical buildings and cultural heritage is like reading a book about the development of Chinese architecture in modern times.

The credit should be given to Tianjin Municipal Committee of the CPC, Tianjin Municipal Government, the authorities of historic relics and historical building preservation and the hardworking efforts made by the related experts and scholars. In 2005, the Regulations on the Protection of Tianjin City's Historic and Stylistic Architecture was established to standardize the renovation of the buildings. A large group of historical buildings that were not listed as cultural relic protection units yet were protected and became a key component of Tianjin cultural heritage. Meanwhile, the renovated historical buildings can be effectively protected and inherited, and also be beneficial to people of our times. In such a way, the memories of architectural culture of the city will go on.

Hopefully, people can learn the historical buildings of Tianjin from this series touch them and feel them. I sincerely hope that the protection of historical buildings will thrive nationwide and that *Historic Architecture in Tianjin* will set an example for the protection and study of cultural heritages of the country.

**Shan Jixiang**
**Head of the State Bureau of Cultural Relics**
**April, 2010**

# 目录
# CONTENTS

# 天津历史风貌建筑概况

天津市历史风貌建筑保护专家咨询委员会第一、第二、第三届主任
天津市规划和自然资源局一级巡视员
路红

## 一、基本情况

历史风貌建筑是天津保护特定建筑遗产的法定名词，按照《天津市历史风貌建筑保护条例》的定位，历史风貌建筑是："建成50年以上，在建筑样式、结构、施工工艺和工程技术等方面具有建筑艺术特色和科学价值；反映本市历史文化和民俗传统特点，具有时代特色和地域特色；具有异国建筑风格特点；著名建筑师的代表作品；在革命发展史上具有特殊纪念意义；在产业发展史上具有代表性的作坊、商铺、厂房和仓库；名人故居及其他具有特殊历史意义的建筑[①]"。

2005年9月1日，《天津市历史风貌建筑保护条例》出台，按照《条例》的规定，经天津市历史风貌建筑保护专家咨询委员会审查，天津市政府于2005–2013年分6批确认了历史风貌建筑877幢、126万平方米。其中，特殊保护级别69幢，重点保护级别205幢，一般保护级别603幢，分布在全市15个区县。在877幢历史风貌建筑中，有各级文物保护单位195处。

1986年天津市被确定为国家级历史文化名城，2006年3月国务院批准的天津市城市总体规划的历史文化名城规划中，确定了14片历史文化街区，大部分历史风貌建筑就坐落在这些历史文化街区内。

天津现存的历史风貌建筑既有中国传统风格的四合院、殿堂、寺院，又有西洋古典、现代建筑，它们和历史文化风貌保护区一起，形成了独特的建筑文化和城市景观，也是天津作为国家级历史文化名城的重要载体。

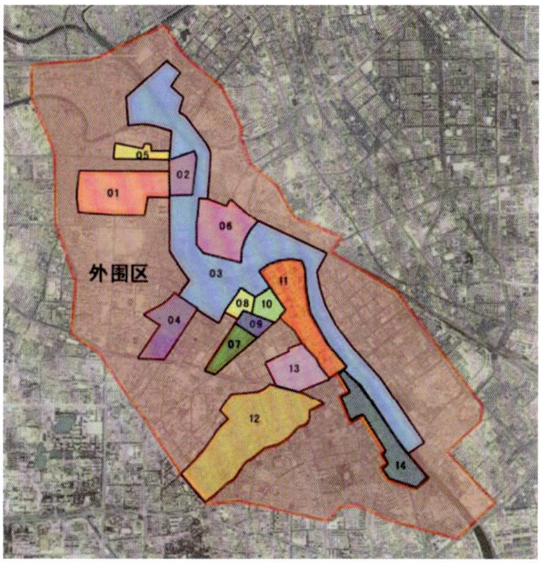


14片历史文化图
14 protective areas of historical and cultural heritages

| | |
|---|---|
| 01. 老城厢历史文化街区 | Seat of the Old City Area |
| 02. 古文化街历史文化街区 | Ancient Cultural Street Area |
| 03. 海河历史文化街区 | Haihe River Area |
| 04. 鞍山道历史文化街区 | Anshan Avenue Area |
| 05. 估衣街历史文化街区 | Gu Yi Street Area |
| 06. 一宫花园历史文化街区 | Yigong Garden Area |
| 07. 赤峰道历史文化街区 | Chifeng Avenue Area |
| 08. 劝业场历史文化街区 | Quan ye cheng Mall Area |
| 09. 中心花园历史文化街区 | Central Garden Area |
| 10. 承德道历史文化街区 | Chengde Avenue Area |
| 11. 解放北路历史文化街区 | North Jiefang Road Area |
| 12. 五大道历史文化街区 | The Five Avenues Area |
| 13. 泰安道历史文化街区 | Taian Avenue Area |
| 14. 解放南路历史文化街区 | South Jiefang Road Area |

① 天津市《天津市历史风貌建筑保护条例》

## 二、历史背景

天津的历史风貌建筑和历史风貌保护区是天津社会和城市发展的见证。天津地区发现最早的人类活动遗存，属距今一万年前的旧石器时代[①]；隋唐、宋辽时期，天津地区出现了规模较大的建筑群。目前人类建筑活动的最早实物为重建于辽代统和二年（984年）的独乐寺。明永乐二年（1404年）天津设卫，明成祖朱棣为纪念自己南下夺取政权之事，赐名“天津”，即天子的渡口，由此开始了天津的城市历史。

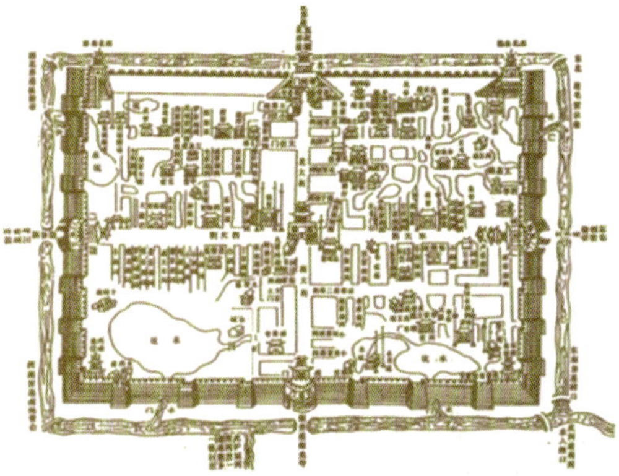

天津老城厢图
The map of the old town of Tianjin

明代鼓楼
The Drum Tower of Ming Dynasty

历经明清两朝，天津以老城厢为建筑的大本营，以漕运文化为基础，经历了由卫城到州城、府城的升级，也逐渐地由单纯的军事基地演变成为商贾云集的中国北方经济文化重镇。天津老城城池为长方形，占地约1.76平方千米，与中国传统古城基本类似，平面是以鼓楼为中心的十字街布局，四条大道两侧配以小街、小巷，形成若干胡同街坊，老城建筑除少数公署衙门、文庙等为传统大式建筑外，民居以小式建筑为主，杂以部分南方民居形式，呈现了南北交融的中国传统建筑风格。

1860年第二次鸦片战争后，天津被迫开埠；1900年八国联军入侵，天津老城于1900年11月26日被八国联军拆毁，四段城墙改成了四条马路。从1860年开始，英、法、美、德、日、俄、意大利、比利时、奥匈帝国等9个帝国主义国家先后在天津设立了租界，天津九国租界的形成大致分为三个阶段。

第一阶段：英、法、美租界的开辟。1860年，英法联军发动的第二次鸦片战争迫使清政府签订了中英、中法《北京条约》，天津开埠成为通商口岸。同年12月7日，划海河西岸紫竹林、下园一带为英租界；次年6月，法、美两国亦在英租界南北分别设立租界。

第二阶段：德、日租界的开辟与英租界的扩张。首先，德国于1895年在海河西岸开辟租界。1896年日本在法租界以西开辟租界。1897年，英国强行将其原租界扩张到南京路北侧。

第三阶段：九国租界的形成。1900年八国联军入侵，俄国于1900年在海河东岸划定租界，比利时于1902年在俄租界之南划租界地，意大利也于同年在俄租界之北开辟租界，最后奥匈帝国在意租界以北占地为租界。与此同时，英、法、日、德四国又趁

① 天津古代建筑［M］. 天津：天津科学技术出版社，1989.

机扩充其租界地，最后形成了九国租界聚集海河两岸，总计占地23 350.5亩（约1 556.7公顷）的格局。而当时的天津老城厢占地2 940亩（约196公顷），仅为租界地的1/8。

九国租界在天津存续时间最长的为英租界——85年，最短的为奥匈租界——17年。九国租界并存同一城市，在世界城市的发展史上是空前的。由此可见天津在中国近代史上负载了最沉重的耻辱，同时九国租界遗存的历史风貌建筑及其建设过程中派生的多元文化，也成为今天城市建设中不可忽视的历史文脉和宝贵的文化资源。大规模的租界建设，使得西洋建筑文化和技术涌入天津，天津的建筑从中国传统形式走向了中西荟萃、百花齐放的形式。

在中国城市发展史上，600年的城市仍是年轻的城市。天津作为国家级历史文化名城，没有北京、西安、南京等古都的显赫地位，也没有扬州、苏州、开封等古城的辉煌文化，天津城市文化的突出价值在于近代百年与西方文明的对接，鸦片战争后中国发生的重大历史事件大部分能在天津找到痕迹，因此在中国史学界，素有“五千年看西安，一千年看北京，近代中国看天津” 的说法。

**三、基本类型**

天津的历史风貌建筑林林总总，跨越了1 000多年，涵盖了居住、公共建筑等多个领域。为便于管理和研究，我们从三个方面进行分类。

（一）按建筑年代分类

1860年第二次鸦片战争后，天津被迫开埠，逐渐成为9个帝国主义国家的租界，天津的建筑从中国式传统建筑走向了中西荟萃，突出地表现了时代的变迁和观念的转换，有很强的时代标记。因此我们以1860年为分水岭，将天津的历史风貌建筑主要分为古代历史风貌建筑（1860年以前）和近代历史风貌建筑（1860–1950年）。

古代历史风貌建筑主要为中国传统式建筑，现存50余幢，主要分布在蓟州、老城厢。如建于辽代统和二年（984年）的独乐

广东会馆
The Guangdong provincial guildhall

寺、元朝泰定三年（1326年）的天后宫、明朝初年（1427年）的玉皇阁。

近代历史风貌建筑是天津历史风貌建筑中数量最多、最具特色的瑰宝，主要分布在天津市中心城区海河两岸。

（二）按使用功能分为十类

居住建筑是目前保存量最大也最具特色的一类，其中又可细分为独立式住宅、单元公寓式住宅、独门联排式住宅等。其他类型为教育建筑、金融建筑、商贸建筑、办公建筑、厂房仓库、宗教建筑、娱乐体育建筑、医院建筑、交通建筑等。

（三）按建筑的外部特征分为五类

中国传统官式建筑：指严格按照中国传统建筑的形制建造的建筑，主要为寺庙、官衙等，如天后宫、玉皇阁、大悲院等。

欧洲古典复兴主义特征：建筑多以古希腊、古罗马及文艺复兴时期的建筑范式为摹本，如原开滦矿务局办公楼、原汇丰银行等。

折中主义特征：既有欧洲典型的集仿主义建筑，又有中西合璧的折中主义建筑，天津大多数历史风貌建筑属于此类，如鲍贵卿旧宅等。

各国民居特征：由中国传统民居和天津地方文化结合产生的天津合院民居形式，如石家大院、徐家大院等；更多的是采用欧洲各国的典型民居形式，如西班牙、英国、德国、意大利等国的民居。

现代主义特征：引进新结构、新材料的建筑，如利华大楼、渤海大楼等。

**四、基本特点**

（一）建筑年代相对集中

天津60%的历史风貌建筑是在1900–1937 年不到40年的时间里建成的。

（二）各类建筑相对集中，呈现群区性

中国传统建筑集中在老城厢和古文化街一带；建筑规模宏大的金融建筑主要集中在解放北路一带，被称为“金融一条

独门独院住宅——张园
A separated mansion — Zhangyuan Garden

单元公寓式住宅——民园大楼
An apartment building — the Minyuan Building

独门联排式住宅——安乐邨
A suite of flats with separated entrances in a block — Anle Village

鲍贵卿旧宅
The former residence of Bao Guiqing

街"；商贸性建筑主要集中在和平路及估衣街、古文化街一带；居住建筑主要集中在老城厢、河北区一宫、河西区大营门、和平区五大道地区及中心花园附近；仓库建筑则集中在海河沿岸。

（三）近代历史风貌建筑的设计理念、应用技术与西方社会同步

一是先进的设计理念：20世纪20年代，正值英国"花园城市"规划理论盛行之时，英租界新区（即现在的五大道地区）基本按照该理论进行规划与建设，居住区规模适中，配备了学校、教堂、花园、体育场等完整的公共配套设施，形成了宜人的空间尺度和舒适的居住环境。新型公寓建筑、联排住宅等也直接从其诞生地移植到了天津。

二是完善的公共配套和室内设施：各租界的建设注重整地筑路，建设完善的市政设施，如路灯、绿化、排水等设施的建设，在住宅中引进推广了水冲式厕所，改善了居住环境，提高了卫生水平。

三是先进的房地产开发模式：各租界的建设引进了西方的房地产开发理念和模式。如英法租界将地块按照四方块划分，周围用道路围合，利于分期出让土地。

四是现代生活方式和城市空间：各租界的建设引进了西方的现代生活方式，如以起居、餐厅、舞厅为中心的家庭生活方式，以公园、教堂、市政厅为中心的社会生活方式，以电车、汽车代步的现代交通方式。这些开放的生活方式与封闭的中国传统方式迥然不同，同时也带来了截然不同的城市空间。

（四）建筑风格纷呈，建筑艺术多样

由于受中国传统建筑和西方建筑思潮的双重影响，形成了中国传统建筑、古典复兴建筑、折中主义建筑、现代建筑等不同风格建筑共存的局面。它们相互辉映，共同形成了天津独特而又丰富的城市空间和景观。

（五）建筑材料及建造技术特色突出

天津独特的地理环境和水土，形成了独特的建筑材料和建造技术，这些材料和技术在历史风貌建筑上得到了充分体现。如黏土过火砖（俗称"疙瘩砖"）在五大道民居中运用广泛，其

达文士小楼（西班牙风格）
The Davinci villa (Spanish style)

许氏住宅（英国风格）
The Xu's Family residence (British style)

利华大楼
Leopold Building

厚重的质感和沉稳的色彩，成为天津建筑的标志。其他如清水砖、粗面石材、仿石水刷石、水泥拉毛墙、细卵石墙等材料也很常见，材料的质感与美感体现了天津建筑的纯朴与厚重。建造技术融会了中国南北、世界东西的技术，形成了天津的特色建造技术。如广东会馆戏楼独特而适用的鸡笼斗拱、石家大院的地下通道式的土空调等都为创新之举。

（六）人文资源丰厚

由于天津靠近北京，开放较早，经济繁荣，社会各界名流涌居天津，天津为他们提供了施展才华的舞台，近代中国上演的历史活剧给天津留下了珍贵的遗迹。经考证，近代有200余位名人政要曾在天津留下了寓所、足迹和故事：革命先驱孙中山、周恩来、邓颖超、张太雷等在此留下了革命斗争的历史；爱国将领张学良、吉鸿昌、张自忠曾将这里作为人生的重要舞台；中国近代史上一批杰出的文教科技界人士梁启超、李叔同、严复、张伯苓、侯德榜等在此创办新学、宣传新文化、实践科技救国的史迹；末代皇帝溥仪、庆亲王载振在这里做过复辟清王朝的白日梦；北洋政府五位大总统袁世凯、徐世昌、黎元洪、冯国璋、曹锟及数任总理和国务大臣在天津上演了一幕幕政治活剧。

伴随这些历史人物，在天津的历史风貌建筑里发生了很多中国近代史的开创性历史事件。曾有学者做过统计，近代中国历史上有130余项"第一"在天津诞生，如第一枚邮票、第一张报纸、第一所现代大学等。这些都构成了天津丰富独特的城市人文和旅游资源。

党的十九大报告指出"加强文物保护利用和文化遗产保护传承"，天津市第十一次党代会报告提出了"着力留住城市之根，加强城市修补和历史风貌建筑保护，挖掘用好丰厚的老城资源，精心打造具有浓厚津味儿的特色街区，延续天津特有的城市发展基因"的要求，这些重要指示为天津历史风貌建筑保护工作指明了方向。我们将进一步集国内外保护经验之长，深入思考保护方向，继续加大保护力度，汇集政府、专家、公众等多方力量，共同守住天津的文脉，为"美丽天津"建设注入重要的历史文化元素；致力于让历史风貌建筑在当今社会"活"起来，使其价值惠及当今社会，惠及广大百姓。

疙瘩砖细部
Details of bricks with coarse and lump surface

细卵石墙面
Pea pebble wall

南开学校
Nankai High School

北洋大学
Peiyang University

# A SUMMARY OF THE HISTORIC ARCHITECTURE IN TIANJIN

Lu Hong

The Fist-level Inspector of Tianjin Bureau of Planning and Natural Resorces

The Director of the first,second,third Session of Tianjin City Historic And Stylistic Constructions Protective Committee

**1. General Description**

According to the *Protective Regulations on the Tianjin City Historic and Stylistic Architecture (Regulations)* , historic and stylistic architecture is a term referring to any constructions and buildings that have been built for more than 50 years, bearing some architectural features or scientific values in terms of their styles, structures, technical skills, or engineering technologies; reflect the city's historical and cultural or traditional folkway and customs being times or local characteristics; or have present distinguished architectural styles of foreign countries; or refer to the representative construction product of any well-known architects; or have special significance in the revolutionary history; or are those representative workshops, business shops, factories and warehouses in the development of the industry; or are the residences of celebrities as well as other constructions of special historical significance. [①]Those streets or districts where such historic constructions are densely built are called historic and stylistic constructions communities or quarters.

The *Regulations* came into force on the first of September, 2005. According to it, and after the authentication of Tianjin Professional Consulting Committee for the Protection of Historic Architecture, the government confirmed 877 historic constructions in six groups, totaling an area of 1,260,000 m$^2$. during the period from 2005 to 2013. Of them, 69 buildings are classified as special important ones to be protected, 205 as key ones and 603 as general ones, all distributed across the 15 districts and counties of the city. Of the 877 buildings, there are 195 relic units of different levels.

Tianjin was confirmed as the national-level historic and cultural city in 1986. In March 2006, the State Council approved the city's overall program including the famous historic and cultural city program, in which 14 historic and cultural landscape protective areas were confirmed, and the majority of the historic and stylistic buildings are situated within these protective areas of historic and cultural heritage.

The existing historic constructions include either those quadrangle compounds, guildhalls and temples, all of traditional Chinese styles, or Western classic and modern architecture. Together with those historical and cultural landscape areas, they have formed a unique architectural culture and city spectacle, thus making up the important part of Tianjin City, a national famous historic and cultural city in China.

Note①: The Protective Regulations on the Tianjin City Historic and Stylistic Architecture.

## 2. Historical Background

The historic and stylistic constructions and such quarters witnessed the development of the city itself and the society. The earliest relics of human existence left over by our forefathers in the Tianjin area can date back to 10,000 years ago during the Old Stone Age. ①During the Sui and Tang, or Song and Liao Dynasties, larger groups of constructions appeared in this area. So far, the earliest construction in ancient times we have found is the Dule Temple, which was reconstructed in the second year of the Tonghe period of the reign of Emperor Shengzong of Liao Dynasty (984). In the second year of the Yongle period of the reign of the Ming Emperor Chengzu (1404), a guard was established, called "Tianjin", a name given by Emperor Chengzu (Zhu Di) himself to mark his expedition to the south to seize the state power. Tianjin means the ferry, specially for the emperor. Since then, the history of the city has begun.

Through the Ming and Qing Dynasties, Tianjin took the seat of the old town as its base for construction. Depending on the Canal Culture, the town developed itself from a guard to a sub-prefecture, and then prefecture, or from a simple military guard post to an important township of business and culture in the north China, with businessmen bustling about at that time. The old town was a rectangle in shape, covering an area of about 1.76 $km^2$, similar to the old towns in ancient China. It was centered on the Drum Tower; streets were laid out in the shape of a cross; along each of the four streets, small lanes or alleys were formed. Except a few constructions of governmental offices or temples of Confucius, which were usually of traditional grandeur structure, the residences of common people were mostly small houses, mixed up partly with the southern-style dwelling houses, presenting a combined style of the traditional houses in the south and the north.

After the Second Opium War in 1860, Tianjin was forced to lend its port to foreign powers. In 1900, the Eight-Power Allied Forces encroached on Tianjin. The old city was destroyed by the forces on November 26 of the same year. Four sections of the city wall were demolished and turned to be four avenues. Since 1860, nine imperialist countries including Britain, France, the United States, Germany, Japan, Russia, Italy, Belgium, and Austria-Hungary acquired the right to supposedly lease a tract of land as concessions in the city one after another. The concessions were formed through three stages.

The first stage: The city ceded tracts of land for concessions to Britain, France and the United States. In 1860, the British-French Allied Forces waged the Second Opium War against China and forced the Chinese Government to sign the *Sino-British Treaty of Beijing* and the *Sino-French Treaty of Beijing* respectively. Tianjin was lent to them to be a port for trade. On December 7th that year, a part of the area on the west bank of the Haihe River including the Purple Bamboo Grove and Xia Yuan Garden was ceded to Britain as its concession in the city. In June, the following year, France and the United States had their concessions on the south and north sides of the area of the British concessions respectively.

The second stage: Germany and Japan seized their concessions and the British concession was expanded. First, Germany acquired its concession on the west bank of the Haihe River in 1895. Then in 1896, Japan had its concession on the west of the

Note①: The Ancient Constructions in Tianjin[M]. Tianjin: Tianjin Scientific and Technological Press.1989.

French concession. In 1897, Britain arbitrarily expanded the area of its former concession to the north side of the Nanjing Road.

The third stage: The formation of the concessions of the nine countries. In 1900, when the Eight-Power Allied Forces encroached on China, Russia got its concession on the east bank of the Haihe River in 1900, on the south side of which, Belgium seized the area as its concession in 1902. In the same year, Italy had its concession on the north side of the Russia's concession. On the north side of the Italy's concession, a part of the area was seized by Austria-Hungary as its concession. At the same time, Britain, France, Japan and Germany seized the opportunity to expand the area of their concessions. Eventually, all the concessions were concentrated on the both sides of the Haihe River, covering 23,350.5 mu of land (about 1,556.7 hectares). At that time, the seat of the old city only occupied 2,940 mu of land (about 196 hectares), equal to one-eighths of the total area of the concessions.

British concession had been maintained for 85 years—the longest period of all. The Austria-Hungary's concession lasted only 17 years—the shortest. This phenomenon in the history of world's cities has never seen before. Accordingly, Tianjin has suffered the galling shame and humiliation in the modern history of China. Meanwhile, the historic and stylistic constructions together with their multi-culture derived from therein, have become important historic context and valuable cultural resources that cannot be neglected in the city construction. The mushrooming of constructions in the area of concessions brought western architectural culture and technologies into Tianjin as torrents. Architecture of the city developed from its traditional Chinese style to the combination of the Chinese and western styles, triggering off a thriving development of all kinds of styles and fashions in the construction industry.

In the history of Chinese cities, a city that has a history of 600 years is still regarded as a young city. As a national famous historic city, Tianjin, though neither having the prominent position in history of such antique capitals as Beijing, Xi'an and Nanjing, nor the brilliant culture as the cities of Yangzhou, Suzhou, and Kaifeng, boasts its own value in terms of cultural interchanges between itself and the western countries over the past hundred years. After the Opium War, some of the vestiges of almost all the historical significant events in China can be found in the city. So, in the Chinese historical circles, a prevalent saying goes: "Xi'an is a witness of the past five thousand years, and Beijing, a witness of the past 1,000 years, while Tianjin, a witness of the past 100 years."

**3. Types of Constructions**

The numerous historic constructions in Tianjin have lasted for more than 1,000 years, including dwelling houses, public constructions and warehouse. For convenient management and study, they can be classified into three categories.

1) Constructions Built in Chronological Order

After the Second Opium War in 1860, Tianjin was forced to lend its port to foreign countries and gradually to cede its tracts of land to nine imperialist countries as concessions, and the construction in the city developed itself from the traditional Chinese style to a combination of the Chinese and Western styles, marking a great change of times and the ideas with a distinctive symbol. Therefore, taking the year 1860 as the watershed, we can classify the historic constructions as the ancient ones (before 1860) and the modern ones (1860-1950).

The ancient ones mainly include traditional Chinese-style architecture. So far, only about 50 such constructions have been left over, most of which are distributed in Jizhou, and the seat of the old city, such as the Dule Temple of Liao Dynasty (built in 984), the Temple for Queen of Heaven of Yuan Dynasty (built in 1326) and the Taoist Temple of Jade Emperor of Ming Dynasty (built in 1427).

The modern ones are treasures of the city with the largest quantity and the most distinctive characteristics, mainly distributed on the both sides of the Haihe River in the downtown of the city.

2) Constructions Classified into Ten Categories by Functions

Dwelling houses are the most in quantity, with most distinctive characteristics. Of these houses, some can be further classified as separated courtyard or compound mansions, flat or apartment and apartment in a block. Other types include school constructions, banking constructions, business and trading headquarters, office buildings, factories and warehouses, churches, entertainment and sports facilities, hospitals, communication facilities.

3) Constructions Classified into Five Categories by Exterior Features

Traditional Chinese bureaucratic constructions: They were built strictly in accordance with the traditional type and system of the officialdom, mainly including temples, government offices, such as the Temple for Queen of Heaven, Taoist Temple and of Jade Emperor, Compound of Great Mercy.

European classic renaissance styled constructions: Most of such constructions were modeled after the constructions of ancient Greece and Rome and those were built during the period of Renaissance, such as the office building of Kailuan Mining Administration , Former Hongkong and Shanghai Bank Corporation.

Eclectic styled constructions: These are combinations of buildings modeling on typical European classic styles and the eclectic patterns together with both the Chinese and western styles. Most constructions in the city can be grouped into this category, such as the former residences of Bao Guiqing.

Dwelling houses of common people: They include traditional Chinese styled common houses and the local courtyard-styled compounds such as Shi's Family compound, and Xu's Family compound. Many other living houses were modeled after the typical European-styled houses such as the Spanish-styled, British-styled, German-styled and Italian-styles houses.

Modern houses: These constructions were built with new materials and in new structures, such as Leopold Building and Bohai Building.

4. Basic Characteristics

1) Constructions being built in a comparatively concentrated period of time. About 60 percent of all the historic constructions were built during the period from 1900 to 1937, less than a period of 40 years.

2) Constructions of each type being built in a concentrated area, making up a quarter of buildings. Traditional Chinese style constructions were concentrated on the seat of the old city and in the Ancient Culture Street. Banking buildings were mainly densely built in the North Jiefang Road, known as "Financial Avenue". Business and trading buildings were concentrated in the Heping Road and the Gu Yi Street and the Ancient Culture Street. Common dwelling houses were on the seat of the old city, the Yigong Garden of the Hebei District, Dayingmen of the Hexi District, the Fifth Avenue of the Heping District and near the Central Garden. Warehouses were mostly built along the banks of the Haihe River.

3) The modern designs and techniques of historic constructions following the patterns of constructions in Western countries, such as the followings.

— Advanced ideas of design: During the 1920s, when the new idea of building a "gardening city" was prevalent in Britain, constructions being built in the new district of the British concession (now the Five Avenues district) at that time were mostly following the practice of this idea. The scope of the residential quarter was moderate, and the quarter was equipped with such facilities as schools, churches and playgrounds, providing a pleasant and comfortable living environment. New model of apartments and flats in a block was also introduced from their origin to Tianjin.

— Complete public support facilities and interior room equipment: All the concessions paid attention to the leveling of ground and construction of roads and perfection of municipal engineering and facilities, such as road lamps, treeplanting, and providing utilities, and flush toilets, so as to improve the living environment and hygienic conditions.

— Advanced idea of development of real estate and property industry: All the concessions introduced the Western idea and patterns in the development of real estate and property, for instance, the British and French concessions divided a tract of land into squares, encircled on four sides by roads, to lend them out at different times.

— Modern way of life and the different city activities: The Western way of life in modern times was introduced into the concessions when they were being built. For instance, the family way of life centered on a living room, a dining room or a ballroom; the public way of life took parks, churches, and the town council as its center of activities; and the people's walking on foot was replaced usually by modern traffic means of trams or automobiles. This modern way of life was quite different from the conservative way of life long time maintained by Chinese people and it also brought in diversified activities in the city.

4) A diversity of construction styles and arts: Influenced by both the traditional Chinese and Western architectural trends of thought, a co-existence situation had been created of the traditional Chinese style, classic renaissance style, eclectic style and modern style. They added radiation and beauty to each other, together presenting a unique and rich city spectacle of Tianjin.

5) Outstanding features of construction materials and techniques: The unique construction materials and techniques must owe to the city's unique geographical environment and its water and soil. These materials and techniques were fully brought into the constructions. For instance, the chamottoe bricks (or known as bricks with coarse gravels on the surface) were widely used in the common houses in the Five Avenues, becoming a special mark of Tianjin's constructions with their solid quality and grave colors.

Other materials like fair-faced bricks, coarse-surfaced slabs, imitation water dressing stones, stucco plastered bricks walls and pea pebbles wall were also used. The constructions introduced techniques from the south and north of China, and the east and west of the world to create the city's unique techniques. For example, the chicken coop-shaped dougong, a traditional Chinese construction technique, was used in the theater stage of Guangdong Guildhall and the self-built underground tunnel conditioner in the Shi's Family compound were all newly created.

6) Affluent humanity resources: Because Tianjin is close to Beijing, and was opened earlier to the outside world, a number of celebrities of society swarmed into the city, where they had opportunities to develop their capabilities and talents. The historical drama staged in modern China has left over precious legacy to the city. According to textual research, about 200 dignified personalities have left over to the city their residences, "footprints" and anecdotes. The revolutionary pioneers like Dr. Sun Yat-sen, Zhou Enlai, Deng Yingchao and Zhang Tailei had led the revolutionary activities in the city; Patriotic generals like Zhang Xueliang, Ji Hongchang, Zhang Zizhong, had regarded Tianjin as a important stage of their lives; scientists and scholars like Liang Qichao, Li Shutong, Yan Fu, Zhang Boling, and Hou Debang, had devoted themselves to the introduction of modern schools, publicity of new cultures, and the practice of salvation of the country by science and technology; Pu Yi, the last emperor of the Qing Dynasty, and Zai Zhen, the imperial prince Qing, had their daydreams of restoration of a dethroned monarch; The five presidents of the Northern Warlord Government (Beiyang Government) Yuan Shikai, Xu Shichang, Li Yuanhong, Feng Guozhang, and Cao Kun and its premiers and ministers of different tenures of office had staged a political farce in the city.

Along with all these historical figures, a number of events of pioneering significance had occurred in these constructions in the modern history of China. According to statistics made by a scholar, about 130 items of inventions originated in the city, including the first postage stamp, the first newspaper, and the first university. They have constituted a part of the city's humanity and tourism resources.

The reports of the 19th National Congress of the Communist Party of China put forward to strengthen the protection and utilization of cultural relics, and the inheritance of cultural heritage. It raised in the reports of the Eleventh Congress of the Chinese Communist Party of Tianjin, the requirements of making efforts to retain the "root" of the city, strengthening the maintenance of the city and conservation of the historic building, exploring deeply and exploiting well the rich and generous old-city resources, elaborately building featured neighborhood with strong Tianjin taste, and remaining the city's development "gene" with Tianjin characteristics, show the direction for the protection of historic architectures in Tianjin. Being open to successful experiences from both home and abroad, we will think deeply into directions for culture protection, will enhance furtherly the protecting efforts and will seek combined forces from the government, the experts and the public; we will strive to jointly keep the cultural and historical context of Tianjin and to inject more historical and cultural elementsin favor of the construction of a "beautiful Tianjin". We will be committed to giving life to those historic architecture and making them to benefit our society as well as a majority of our citizens.

# 天津历史风貌建筑之居住建筑概述

路红① 赵建波②

历史风貌建筑是《天津市历史风貌建筑保护条例》中法定的历史建筑保护名称。目前经天津市政府批准的746幢、114万平方米历史风貌建筑中，居住建筑共有560幢，占75%，共有59万平方米，占52%。无论从数量还是类型上，居住建筑都占据一个显著的位置。大量尺度适宜、外观优美、色彩和谐的居住建筑构成了天津近代城市的重要肌理，也成为毛泽东主席赞誉的"北京四合院，天津小洋楼"中的主角。本文旨在用翔实的资料、比较的方法，对天津历史风貌建筑中的居住建筑进行分析，以期能为关心天津历史风貌建筑的朋友们梳理出分析的脉络，提供欣赏的视角。

## 一、发展脉络

天津现存历史风貌建筑中的居住建筑，建成年代较早的有石家大院（始建于1875年）、徐家大院（十九世纪九十年代）等，建成年代较晚的是利华大楼（1943年）。在近70年的时间跨度里，天津经历了清朝末年、北洋军阀、九国租界、中华民国、抗日战争、解放战争等朝代更替和连年战事，居住建筑的建设发展也受到极大的影响。本文即根据其不同特点总结为四个阶段。

（一）老城—城市居住的传统形态

天津城发端于旧三岔河口地区，地处南北运河、海河等河流的汇合处，受惠于历代航运、漕运，经济发展较快，大约于金元时期就形成了聚落点。明永乐二年（1404年）天津设卫，清雍正三年（1725年）改卫为州，雍正九年（1731年）升州为府。从而逐步形成了天津拱卫京师、北方经济重镇的地位。

明清的天津城是一座典型的中国北方平原城市，面积约1.76平方公里，矩形平面，四周环墙，以鼓楼为中心，道路骨架十字正交。老城厢当时有"北门富、东门贵、南门贫、西门贱"的说法，衙署集中在东西大街以北，居住区多集中在东西大街以南。这个时期的住宅多是传统的北方合院式住宅（如徐家大院）及简易平房。人口密度大，到清道光年间，已有人口近20万。居民分布在旧城区和三岔河口上下的沿河两岸。

1860年天津被迫开放。开埠之初，老城厢仍然延续了昔日的繁荣，商贾云集，就连外国商人多数也居住在旧城中，有的干脆把洋行也设在城里。四条大道两侧配以小街、小巷，形成若干胡同街坊，老城建筑除少数公署衙门、文庙等为传统大式建筑外，民居以小式建筑为主，杂以部分南方民居形式，呈现了南北交融的中国传统建筑风格。在一些住宅的门楼、外檐装饰上，也嫁接了一些西洋建筑符号，体现了"西风渐进"社会潮流。

1900年八国联军侵占天津，破城后公开行抢三日，又纵火烧城，老城历此劫难，元气大伤。后经1912年的"壬子兵变"、及1922年和1924年两次直奉战争的轮番洗劫，更是满目疮痍。有产阶级认为在这里生命和财产都没有保证，遂陆续避入租界，这

① 路红，天津市历史风貌建筑保护专家咨询委员会主任，工学博士，正高级建筑师。
② 赵建波，天津大学建筑学院副教授。工学博士。

里渐渐成为平民区或贫民区，住宅建设多年停滞不前，天津老城厢逐渐走向衰落。

（二）租界—"国中之国"的住宅建设

1860 年，英法联军发动的第二次鸦片战争迫使清政府签订了中英、中法《北京条约》，天津开埠成为通商口岸。同年 12 月 7 日，英国首先在此设立租界，后法、美、德、日、俄、比、意、奥等国相继强划租界，并不断向外扩张。从开始设立到完全形成，租界区的面积扩大到约 14 平方公里，约为天津老城厢面积的八倍。从 1860 年第一个租界建立至 1945 年最后一个租界消亡，在长达 8 5 年的时间里，各帝国主义列强在天津各自的租界，相继设立工部局，分别以他们自己的意图来建设这些"国中之国"。由于缺乏统一全面的规划，而中国人又无力干涉租界区的事务，形成了近代天津城市建设的两面性——一方面城市整体混乱杂糅，另一方面各租界区内规划有序、自有特色。

1、法租界的居住区建设

法租界（1 8 6 0 年—1 9 45 年），占地面积达到 189 公顷。最主要的居住区是与繁华的中街（今解放北路）相邻的劝业场、中心公园一带。

初时，劝业场一带只是一片空地，多水塘、坟茔，地价极贱。1900 年被法租界扩入后，一时仍无多大改观。随着中街的建设，地产投机商们逐渐觉察到该地区的发展前途，土地投机活动日益昌盛，地价陡升数倍，成为地产商的致富法宝。二十年代这一带的商业就已现繁荣，商店、旅馆、饭庄、影院等商业娱乐建筑大量建造，成为天津新兴的商业中心。

在商业娱乐业繁荣的同时，住宅也在其周边相应出现。辛亥革命后，军阀官僚和新兴的资本家纷纷迁往租界区居住，他们不仅建豪宅（多为独立式住宅）供自己享用，还经营成片的新式里弄出租给广大职员以牟利。一些洋行买办及新兴的资本家建宅于环法国花园（今中心公园，图 1）的霞飞路（今花园路），而军阀们则在丰领事路（今赤峰道）两侧营造私宅，最多时赤峰道共聚集了十几位民国督军，被称为督军街。这个时期，受上海新石库门里弄的影响，法租界也开始建造新式里弄住宅。

2、英租界的居住区建设

英租界（1860—1943）占地面积达到 410 公顷，是九国租界中设立最早、面积最大的租界，主要的居住区是英租界新区（今五大道地区）和泰安道地区。

十九世纪八十年代，海河逐渐淤塞，严重地影响了天津航运的发展。而各租界国的利益，与海河的通畅与否息息相关。因此，1897 年专门成立了海河工程局，负责疏浚改造海河的下游航道，全面整治海河。1902 年至 1923 年这二十多年里，共六次对海河挖泥清淤，裁弯取直，使上下游河床普遍刷深拓宽，航道畅通。1927 年以前，2000 吨级的轮船可沿海河

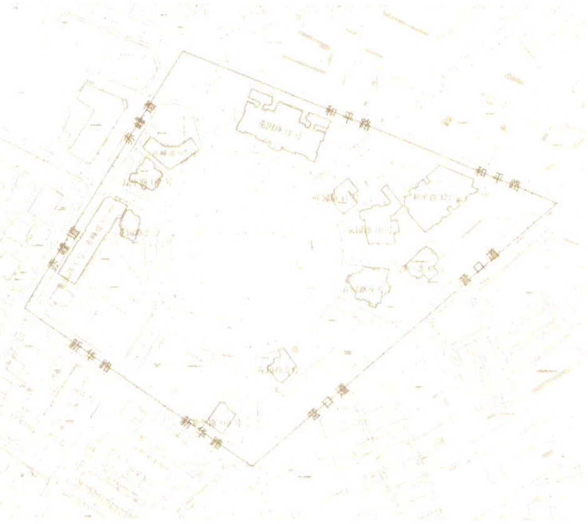

图1 中心花园（原法国花园）平面图
Fig.1 Layout of the Central Park (the former French Park)

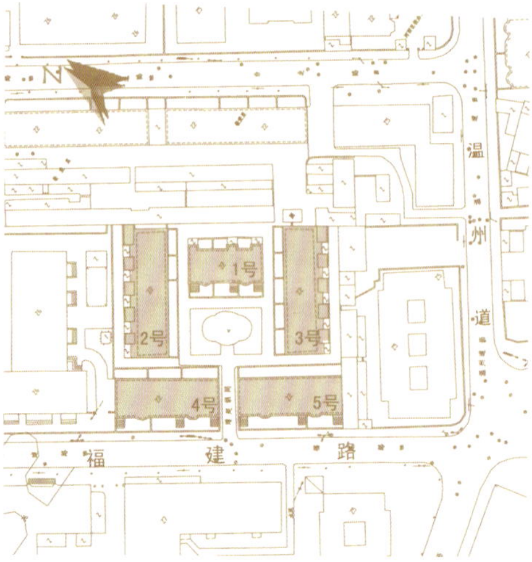


图2 增延胡同平面图
Fig.3 Site plan of Zengyan Lane

直接抵达市区。与此同时，每次疏浚所挖出的大量泥沙则用铁管输送到低洼沼泽地带用来填平垫高，即所谓的“吹泥填地”。

英租界新区—即1902年英租界向墙子河(现南京路)外侧推广所占的近267公顷土地，原属低洼的沼泽，在20世纪初的“吹泥填地”中得到了很大的改善，这给英租界的建设提供了空间上的可能。从1906年开始到1928年这一阶段，新区处于市政建设阶段，基本上是整地筑路，敷建市政设施，也有部分住宅建设，主要以独立式住宅为主。1928年后，住宅进入成片开发阶段，建设速度加大，除独立式住宅外，新式里弄住宅、集合式公寓住宅也全面开花，使其迅速成为高级居住区。

英租界新区是专门为建设高级居住区而设，二十世纪二十年代，正值英国“花园城市”规划理论盛行之时，因此英租界新区的规划、建设基本按照该理论进行规划与建设，非常有特色。例如居住区规模适中，配备了学校、教堂、花园、体育场等完整的公共配套设施，形成了宜人的空间尺度和舒适的居住环境。为保证该居住区的环境质量，不设商业中心，并禁止电车等公共交通车辆进入，因而该区域的道路规模较小，尺度宜人。新型集合式公寓住宅、新式里弄、联排住宅等也直接从其诞生地移植到了天津。在建设中注重整地筑路，建设完善的市政设施，如路灯、绿化、上下水等设施的建设，在住宅中引进推广了水冲式厕所，改善了居住环境，提高了卫生水平。在建设中引进了西方的房地产开发观念和模式。将地块按照四方块划分，周围用道路围合，利于分期出让土地。由于英租界“严格规定必须是外国式的建筑，营造计划必须先送工部局批准。虽然建筑必须是外国式的，但是，住户是不限国籍的。”[①]因此，居住区内建筑形式多样，均具异域特征。

由于英租界新区的居住环境优越，不仅吸引了许多官僚、资本家及下野政客来此建宅或租屋居住，就连原来居住在河北新区和劝业场一带的中上层人士也纷纷迁入，在短短的几年内就形成了由今马场道、睦南道、大理道、常德道及重庆道为骨干的“五大道”高级居住区，是当时天津高级住宅建设最集中的地区。

3、意租界的居住区建设

意租界（1902—1945年），占地面积为51.4公顷。意租界内，除设置兵营、领事馆、工部局等公共设施外，很少有商业建筑，主要为居住区（今一宫花园地区）。

意租界的道路规整，而且影楼剧场、烟馆妓院都比较少，环境整洁幽静，下野军阀、失意政客纷纷相中这块风水宝地，视其为“世外桃源”，皆纷至沓来，在此兴建了大量的别墅，故此意租界建筑是以花园别墅式居住建筑为主。如梁启超先生的旧宅（1914年建）及饮冰室书斋（1924年建）、奉系军阀汤玉麟的府邸（1912年建）以及民族路花园住宅等。意租界除建有多座独立式高级住宅以外，还有一些新式里弄住宅，如1923年建造的团结西胡同，1926年建造的团结东胡同等。

由于意国工部局对建筑管理非常严格，如当时规定沿街建筑物立面不许雷同，所以现存的意租界建筑式样很多，临街寓所形象尤佳，几条主要街面景观也各具特色，比较集中地反映在民族路、自由道、民生路等干道上。

4、奥匈租界的居住区建设

奥匈租界（1902—1917年），占地面积为68.7公顷。奥匈租界建设时间较短，其建设方法基本与相邻的意租界一致。邻海河的地段早期以公共建筑建设为主，如俱乐部、领事馆等。后期开始住宅建设。一战后，奥匈帝国作为战败国，归还了租界，住宅建设仍继续进行。现遗存的住宅形式有独立式住宅，如袁氏旧居、鲍贵卿旧居等，又有新式里弄住宅，如冯国璋旧居等。

5、德租界的居住区建设

德租界（1895—1917年），占地面积为280公顷。德租界沿海河、解放南路发展，沿河除码头仓库外，以独立式住宅为主，可近眺海河风光。沿解放南路两侧布置德国俱乐部、德国领事馆、德国兵营等公共建筑，内侧布置居住区，形成了以小白楼为中心的商业居住混合区、以福建路、台湾路一带为代表的居住区。住宅形式除独立式住宅外，出现了大量的新式里弄和围合式组团，如增延胡同（图2），住宅的围合方式和建筑形象与德国本土住宅有很强的传承性，具有较明显的特征。

6、日租界的居住区建设

日租界（1898—1943年），占地面积为143公顷。日租界以平行于海河的旭街（现和平路）为商业中心，垂直于海河的宫

① 杨秉德.[M]//《中国近代城市与建筑》.北京：中国建筑工业出版社.1993, 106.

岛街（现鞍山道）布置行政、军事机构、学校和少量独立式住宅，如静园、张园等。旭街和宫岛街形成的四个地区，旭街以北沿海河的两个地区以商贸为主，以南的两个地区则为居住区，住宅以新式里弄住宅为主。日租界比之英、法、德、意租界，其住宅建设规模不小，但建筑质量较差、建筑单体简单，环境建设上带有明显的东方意识。目前日租界存留的历史风貌建筑较少。

7、其他租界的居住区建设

俄租界（1900—1924 年），占地面积为 365 公顷。俄租界面积较大，但由于国内形势动荡，资金缺乏，俄租界建设较少。目前，仅留下原俄国领事馆、兵营等建筑，在现十三经路小王庄一带，存留部分居住建筑。

美租界（1860—1902 年），占地面积为 8.7 公顷。美国一直将租界交给英国管理，后期又卖给英国。美租界基本以公共建筑为主，如英国俱乐部、招商局、泰莱饭店等。

比租界（1902—1931 年），占地面积为 49 公顷。比租界基本用作码头仓储和堆栈。

（三）河北新区—城市发展的新契机

十九世纪末，京奉铁路通车后，先期建成的火车站（老龙头车站，今天津东站），处于奥匈、意、俄三国租界的包围之中。清政府为了在商业交通上能与外来势力竞争，推行新政，着手建设“河北新区”。1903 年在新开河地段建设新车站，即今北站，同时开辟今中山路至新开河一带的新区；在完善新区经纬道路系统的基础上，陆续兴办工厂，开设学堂，督造衙署，成立会所等，使其逐渐成为天津新兴的工商业中心，占地约 6.534 平方公里。

辛亥革命后，河北新区成为北洋军阀政府所在地，北洋实业界的许多厂家也都设厂于此，这一带的政府机关人员和铁路工商业职工人数骤增，河北新区的住宅建设从此进入全面繁荣阶段。一些军阀、官商瞅准机会，纷纷在此购地置屋，出租谋利。此时的居住建筑以院落式里弄住宅为主，服务对象多是城市中下层居民，还有一些简陋的工房，主要为新涌进城市的产业工人居住，如北洋工房。住宅的经营者也多属中国本土房地产商。1928 年以后，随着北洋军阀统治的结束，河北新区渐趋没落。租界区的繁荣以及新式里弄住宅的出现，导致院落式里弄的销声匿迹。

河北新区的建设，可以视为二十世纪初叶中国与帝国主义列强的分庭抗礼之争，其业绩不可忽视，但终因北洋军阀的内耗，导致了最终的失败。

（四）南市开发—租界与老城的边缘地带

南市位于旧城区以南，日租界以西，原是一片无人居住的荒地。1903 年日本扩充租界时称其为“预备居留地”，致使中国政府长期失管，因而有“三不管”之称。

随着日租界旭街（今和平路北段）的逐步繁荣，这一城市繁华区边缘地带的潜在经济价值日益明显。觉察到这一点，许多豪贵也就在此购买土地，经营房产。如江苏督军李纯经营的东兴公司，江西督军陈光远的振德房产公司，荣源等人开设的荣业房产公司等。这一阶段南市除继续建造部分院落式里弄和简陋的平房外，还出现了一些早期石库门里弄住宅—天津俗称“锁头式住宅”。

## 二、基本特点

（一）各个时期居住建筑建设的差异明显

1860 年以前的天津居住建筑，仍然以一家一户自建自住为主。住宅形式以中国北方传统的合院住宅为主，也吸收了部分南方建筑的风格。

而近代天津居住建筑的发展大致可以 1910 年为界，分为两个阶段。早期基本上紧跟着经济中心的迁移而变迁，后来则是以追求居住质量而选择方便、安静的地区，以居住区的形式成规模建设。

开埠之初的旧城区延续了昔日的繁荣，就连来自英、法等国的商人为方便贸易也都居住在城中，住宅形式基本上延续了传统的合院式住宅，虽也有外来的券廊式住宅，但终因气候差异而匿迹。十九世纪末河北新区崛起后，城市的经济和政治中心都转移到那里，大量的院落式里弄住宅适时地出现，成为当时住宅建设比较集中的地区。南市区作为城市经济向边缘的渗透，依旧带来该区域住宅的规模建设，部分房产公司在此建设经营了一批锁头式里弄住宅。劝业场地区后来居上，成为寸土寸金的商业黄金地段，于是在其附近又大量建设了新式里弄住宅，同时也小规模地建造了独立式住宅群。

当经济相对稳定，住宅的建设不再受商业利益的吸引而到处流动，而是选择方便、安静、比较繁荣的地区作为居住区，于是英租界新区、意租界等地区以追求居住的安逸舒适为目标，有目的、有计划地开发住宅。而俄、奥、德、比租界由于以仓储贸易为主，住宅建设很少。

（二）居住模式随社会经济的发展而变化

作为北方重要的通商城市，天津受外来文化的冲击较为严重，经济结构从自然经济向商品经济转轨非常快，这种骤变导致建筑的各个方面迅速发生变化：一方面是传统住宅努力改革以适应新需求，另一方面是外来的生活方式和建筑形式渐被人们效仿和接收。居住模式随着社会变革发生了巨大的变化，并使得居住建筑在建筑形式、功能构成、营造方式等诸多方面出现相应变化。

第一，快速城市化使住宅建设趋向高密度。

天津由开埠之初 1.76 平方公里的小城迅速成长为北方的商业中心，其间不过短短的几十年，在快速城市化的过程中，人口增长非常快。为与迅速发展的城市化过程相适应，必须不断探索与建筑技术水平相适应的高容积率住宅，另外，提高住宅容积率也符合房产商追逐商业利益的目的。因此，脱胎于传统合院式住宅的院落式里弄住宅，逐渐演变为锁头式住宅，继而形成新式里弄。新式里弄源于西方的联排式住宅，它通过增加建筑层数（一般在三层左右）来得到足够的使用空间，舒适性也较好，从而成为近代天津建造量最大的住宅形式。

第二，住宅功能布局与生活方式相适应。

由于近代社会中现代生活方式向传统的渗透，住宅的空间格局和功能构成也相应地发生了变化。传统的合院式住宅，空间格局非常严整，内部各房间大致按位置划分为堂屋、厢房、倒座及耳房，而使用功能与房间之间的对位一般并不固定。受外来生活方式的影响，住宅各房间逐渐根据使用功能来分割，如客厅、起居室、卧室、厨房、餐厅以及储藏间等，后来又出现了车库，房间功能的确定使住宅平面布局要复杂得多。从院落式里弄→锁头式里弄→新式里弄→独立式住宅的发展脉络中明确体现出这种变化过程。

这种生活方式的变化过程在住宅中也留下了一些过渡时期的空间形态—虽然建筑形式和空间构成是西式的，却有许多方面反映了传统生活的缩影。以独立式住宅为例，在英租界庆王府，外观与空间构成均以西式为主，却在加建的三层设有祖先堂，在筑“洋房”的同时又建了中式园林；法租界庄乐峰住宅的附属部分中也布置了佛堂；另外，在天津的锁头式里弄、新式里弄和独立式住宅中，都在主体建筑之后建有附属建筑，供下人居住使用，这明显是受中国传统文化中“尊卑有序”观念和传统四合院建筑空间构成的影响。

第三，近代社会商业化使住宅的营造与经营方式发生转变。

在原有经济模式下，传统的住宅多是居住者个人营造，自己居住，住宅建设速度比较缓慢。随着城市近代化过程的加快，尤其在天津这种以租界占主体的城市中，这种简单的营建与经营模式已不能适应社会发展的需要。以河北新区为例，作为新的经济、政治中心，人员的大量流入需要大批的住宅能够在短时期内完成，于是由房产商统一营造与经营的模式适时出现。当然，早期的房产营造与经营主要是由军阀与官僚把持的，商人的介入则是稍后的事了。这种由房产商统一营造与经营的模式比传统的方式迅速，易于成片开发，与当时的社会发展相适应，并在以后的南市区、劝业场地区以及英租界新区等的建设中得到延用。

（三）租界区建设多于旧城区建设

在天津城市的发展过程中，旧城区面积仅1.76平方公里，老城中房屋密度较大，没有多少发展余地。河北新区的开辟在一定程度上提供了发展空间，也只有6.534平方公里，而九国租界区的面积为14平方公里，将近旧城区面积的八倍。如此大面积的土地不仅被建设成工业仓储和大片的商业区，而且也为居住建筑的发展提供了空间。

近代中国社会一直比较动荡，天灾人祸不断，而租界区内却相对安定，住宅建设从未间断。在租界中，一方面各租界国凭借特殊的租界政策，为在租界中居住的人提供外国法律在政治利益和经济利益方面的保护；另一方面他们为了将天津建设成为华北地区的洋务中心，在租界区内有一定的经济投入，并相应采取了一系列的土地政策和市政措施。这些优势对许多的有产阶级具有很大的吸引力，他们纷纷来此经商、居住或从事房地产业，正是这些有产阶级的经济投入，使租界得以迅速发展。因此，租界区的住宅建设在规模、速度和质量上均远远优于旧城区，表现出近代天津城市住宅发展不平衡的一面。

## 三、近代居住建筑风格特征

（一）单体风格特征

在天津的历史风貌建筑中，近代居住建筑占据了主导地位。近代居住建筑以租界为大本营，其风格特征非常明显，其演进大致可分为三个时期：早期以传统住宅向近代社会的过渡为代表，中期是折中和古典复兴占主流，到后期现代住宅成为发展方向。这三个时期各有其时代背景，各具特色。

早期的租界居住建筑多为券廊式，“大抵模仿香港的，但是香港的建筑形式却是从印度传来的，结果常常是房屋内部宽敞，家具充裕，宜于夏天居住，但一到冬天，却使人一看就感到寒意”[①]。盲目地照搬，却因气候的南北差异而不适用，很快就不再建造。早期的院落式里弄和锁头式里弄住宅，基本上都是在传统居住建筑的格局和形式上借鉴了西方联排式的组合方式，在细部装饰方面不仅有本民族的形式，也吸收了外来的东西。虽也出现了独立式住宅，但为数极少，有钱的人们依然生活在传统的中式住宅中。从整体上看，这一时期的住宅是以传统住宅向近代社会过渡为主，在建筑中所反映的是中西两种文化的对话与融合。

二十世纪二三十年代，恰值西方折中主义、古典复兴思潮盛行，西风东渐，在天津这个帝国主义的远东殖民城市，这种建筑思潮也非常流行。辛亥革命后新兴的民族资产阶级受西方思想文化的影响，生活方式逐步西化，反映在建筑上，常常是猎奇和标新立异，自然而然地接收了在西方风头正劲的折中主义和古典复兴的建筑思潮。这一时期的住宅，大部分采用洋折中、洋古典的方式处理住宅的外观。如原意租界的汤玉麟住宅就是典型的意大利古典复兴建筑，而原英租界的孙殿英住宅在外观上罗列了巴洛克的柱子和花饰、意大利文艺复兴时期府邸常见的挑檐、简洁的金属栏杆等。这种情况不仅限于独立式住宅，在新式里弄住宅中也明显表现出这种风尚，如疙瘩楼就是在地方材料的基础上装饰古典符号，集各种形式于一体。折中与古典的风潮直到二十世纪三十年代后期受现代建筑运动的影响才有所收敛。

二十世纪三十年代后期，现代建筑以其简洁的形式、实用的功能得到普遍认可，后来居上，在天津开始扎根、发展，并迅速渗透到各种住宅形式中。如大兴村、桂林里等里弄式住宅，王占元住宅等独立式住宅，以及香港大楼、民园大楼、茂根大楼等集合式公寓式住宅，而高层办公兼公寓则从一开始就是伴随着现代建筑进入天津的，如利华大楼。一批现代建筑的出现，给天津这个近代城市增添了一抹清新的气息，然而由于战争的升级影响到租界区的安定，建设停滞，现代住宅未能得到充分的发展。

总的来说，天津近代居住建筑风格以折中主义为主，并具有一定的混杂性。因业主的喜好和猎奇的需求，将不同地域、不同时代的东西聚集在同一所住宅上，以建筑师的技巧将其杂糅一处，使其和谐统一。例如，法国花园的章瑞庭住宅，孟莎式屋顶、古典柱式等表明其法式古典建筑的风格，但入口处的半圆形花厅却覆盖比较现代的透明玻璃屋顶，而整幢建筑却丝毫没有

① 杨秉德.[M]//《中国近代城市与建筑》.北京：中国建筑工业出版社.1993, 92.

不协调的感觉，类似的作法在张学铭旧宅中也有出现。

（二）群体风格特征

在近代天津居住建筑发展的后期，房地产经营的成熟使住宅建设相对独立，很快就不再受经济及工业繁荣的影响而迁移，后期多是有规模的区片开发而形成居住区。区片建设形成住宅的群体风貌，这也是天津近代居住建筑风格的一大特征。

近代天津的居住区分布大致呈区片和线状两种形式。住宅比较集中，风貌比较突出，保存较好的区域有五大道居住区、法国花园居住区、意国花园居住区等。其中五大道居住区的住宅形式最为混杂，根据英租界当局规定，只允许建造外国式样的住宅，不允许有中国传统住宅。于是，英式的、意式的、西班牙式的，折中的、古典的、现代的全都粉墨登场，纷纷出现在该地区。而法国花园居住区和意国花园居住区的风貌相对统一，分别是以法式住宅和意式住宅为主，风格典型。线状分布的住宅因其相对集中，也较有特色，如日租界的鞍山道、法租界的赤峰道等。

这些集中在几个较大区域内的住宅形成该区域的风格特色，而几个区域又以其不同的特色共同形成天津近代住宅的风貌特征。天津的这些形式各异、各具特色的住宅包容了不同风格、不同地域的住宅建筑形式，遂有“万国建筑博物馆”之称。

**四、基本类型和典型实例**

天津历史风貌建筑中的居住建筑的类型丰富，形式多样，现从居住形态上分五种类型简介。

（一）中国传统合院式住宅

石家大院

石家大院坐落于西青区杨柳青镇，特殊保护等级历史风貌建筑，现为博物馆。石家为清代津门“八大家”之一，此宅系石家后人石元仕宅第。该建筑为典型的四合院住宅建筑群，始建于1875年。整个院落以“箭道”为中轴，分为东西两部分，共有10个独立的四合院或三合院，房屋二百余间，占地面积约6000平方米，建筑面积约3000平方米，院中的戏楼是我国北方规模较大的民居戏楼。　房屋均为砖木结构，屋顶皆为硬山，起人字脊或元宝脊，外墙为青砖砌筑。砖、木、石雕等建筑装饰工艺精美，造型别致，并借鉴了西方建筑装饰特色，颇具观赏价值。

（二）西式独立式住宅

二十世纪初，独立式住宅的形式传入我国。二十世纪二十年代以后，一些大城市如上海、南京、天津、青岛等地的经济发展比较快，许多外国人、官僚、资本家多是这种居住方式，于是独立式住宅的建设在这些地方形成规模。就天津而言，虽然早在河北新区建设时期就已出现了独立式住宅，但其为数较少，不具代表性。直到二十世纪二十年代末，独立式住宅逐步形成天津近代的“小洋楼”风貌。

独立式住宅在建筑的平面布置、形式、技术和设备上较多吸取了西方的经验，而在内部装修、庭院绿化方面则保存着中国固有的习俗爱好。欧化的技术设备、西方住宅式样和中国旧式的生活方式交织在一起，构成复杂的综合体。它从一个侧面突出地反映了当时社会上层人物的生活特点和思想特点。这种住宅形式大多趋向“新奇”、内容繁杂，花样百出，反映了居住者炫耀个人经济实力和标榜生活情趣的心理；住宅的组成一般均由主体建筑和附属服务部分组成，附属服务部分位于主体建筑之后，这固然是功能分区的结果，但同时也表达了居住者主从有别的阶级观念，等级分明的心理不言自明；而住宅主体空间构成的核心一般是较大面积的厅，多两层贯通，作为公共空间，以适应社交文化的需要，也反映了当时社会上追求西方的生活方式的风气。

1、李吉甫旧宅（图3）

李吉甫曾为天津近代“四大洋行”之一的英商仁记洋行的买办，其住宅位于原法租界花园路12号，是围绕中心花园最大的一幢高级独院式别墅住宅。该住宅建于1918年，由瑞士乐利工程司设计，建筑面积4890平方米。

该住宅坐北朝南，面对中心花园，沿南北向轴线对称布局。主楼为砖木混合结构，地上一层，局部二层，地下一层。由三组建筑围绕方形庭院成“品”字形布置，基地东北及西北两角分设中式附属建筑。

庭院是该建筑空间构成的核心，建筑各部分均围绕庭院空间展开，整体环境景观非常优美。庭院东西两组建筑平面近似方形，均以中部带回廊的方厅为中心，周围有卧室、客厅、餐厅、配餐室、书房、浴厕等房间，并各有一组附属用房与其相接。方厅两层贯通，上覆十字交叉拱顶，拱顶四周设半圆拱窗。中央庭院与两个方厅共同统领整个住宅，是该建筑独特的空间构成，在天津诸多的近代独立式住宅中尚不多见。整幢建筑构图虚实分明。建筑墙身多为红色清水砖墙，局部为水刷石饰面，檐口及窗套饰以古典线脚。

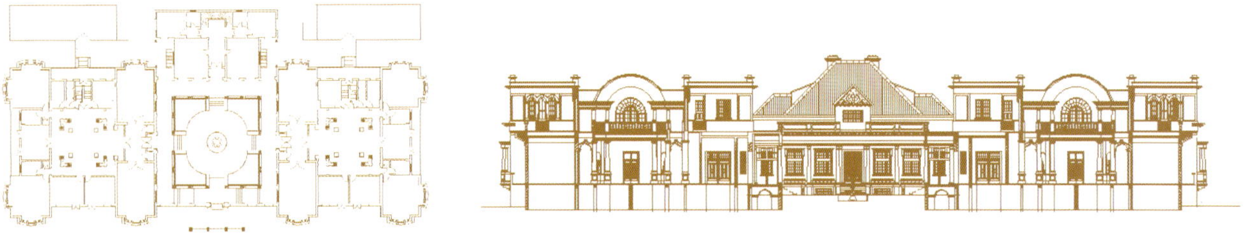

a. 首层平面图 Layout of the First Floor　　b. 剖面图 Section Elevation

图3 李吉甫旧宅 The former residence of Li Jifu

2、民族路原意租界花园住宅（图4）

传统的意大利城市中，广场是其最突出的特征，多数城市都建有壮丽的广场，并以雕像、纪念碑等作为广场的视觉中心。就是远在天津的租界，他们也依然保持着这个传统。花园广场中心立有纪念马可·波罗的科林斯式石柱，柱顶立雕像，柱础饰以石雕，下设喷水池。

1908—1916年，广场周边陆续建设8幢独立式住宅。各住宅的平面布局大同小异：首层为起居室、客厅，二层是卧室，楼梯通道可达屋顶平台。住宅立面采用浅色饰面，入口为爱奥尼克柱式的廊柱，檐口局部挂瓦，自然过渡至女儿墙，临广场处皆高起塔亭。檐下及窗洞上部点缀雕饰。

由于意租界工部局对租界内的建筑要求形式不得雷同，故而各住宅虽风格一致，但形式相近而不相同，就连塔亭也极尽变化。广场与周围的住宅建筑群和谐统一，再现了意大利的城市风貌。

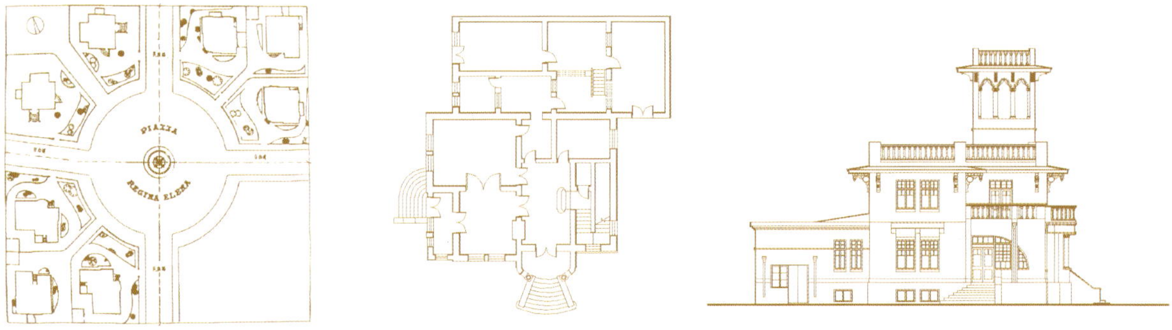


a. 总平面图 Site plan　　b. 首层平面图 Layout of the First Floor　　c. 立面图 Elevation

图4 民族路（原意租界）花园住宅 The Garden house on Minzu Road of the Italian Concession

（三）院落式里弄住宅

院落式里弄住宅源自天津，并以天津为中心向外辐射，在北方地区有一定影响。作为天津早期里弄住宅的主要类型，是在北方传统三合院住宅空间形式的基础上，受西方联排式住宅的影响发展起来的。它吸收了当时西方联排式住宅密集布局的特点，并与当时的社会经济需要相适应，是传统合院式住宅为适应住宅商品化和高密度要求而进行的变通。

通庆里（图5）

通庆里位于南开区古文化街北端东侧，重点保护等级历史风貌建筑，现为商业用房。通庆里建于清末民初，占地面积约1800平方米，建筑面积约2100平方米，为6个独立的院落串联组成的里巷。建筑在里巷出入口处建有过街楼，具有较强的空间归属感。每个院落内相向有两座青砖二层楼房，砖木结构，坡屋顶，首层及二层均建有开敞外廊。建筑功能、风格、装饰和里巷布局既有中国传统建筑元素，又有西洋建筑符号，融合了中国南北方民居的风格，集萃了东西方建筑符号，是天津近代折中主义建筑的代表。

a. 总平面图 Site plan　　b. 立面图 Elevation　　c. 首层平面图 Layout of the First Floor

图5 通庆里 Tong Qing Lane

（四）新式里弄住宅

二十世纪二十年代初，新式里弄住宅在天津出现。早期多集中在法租界劝业场一代，还有一部分建造在意租界内，英租界新区开辟后，这里成为新式里弄住宅最为集中的地区。

新式里弄住宅一般为二层或三层，各分户单元联排布置。单元一般依开间的大小分为单开间、一间半、两开间、两间半以及自由式布局五种类型，其中一间半新式里弄住宅建造量最多。各分户单元中，房间功能分工明确。起居室、卧室、厨房、卫生间以及车库和佣人间在不同层内按功能要求合理分布，每户均有独立的出入口直接对外。结构形式一般仍为砖木混合结构，到后期才少量采用砖混结构。建筑设备较齐全，室内装修朴实。新式里弄住宅比较注意建筑与环境的结合，庭园及弄道内绿化较好，生活环境安宁舒适。室外小院作为空间过渡，宅后设杂物院附属服务。住宅外观往往于同一街区内西方各国风格兼而有之，形式多样，风格迥异。

1、安乐邨（图6）

安乐邨，位于马场道、睦南道与桂林路交叉口附近，1933年由意大利建筑师鲍乃蒂（P.Bonetti）设计，是较高级的联排式新式里弄住宅，其服务对象多为中高级职员。

安乐邨共计三幢，呈周边式与行列式混合布置。弄道宽阔，日照通风良好。各分户单元均有前院与后院，前院为半开敞式

a. 总平面图 Site plan　　b. 首层平面图 Layout of the First Floor　　c. 立面图 Elevation

图6 安乐邨里弄 Anle Village

绿化庭院，后院较小。弄道两侧与各户前院广植树木，生活环境优美舒适。

2、疙瘩楼（图7）

疙瘩楼，坐落在河北路283~295号，建于1937年，由意大利建筑师鲍乃蒂（P. Bonetti）设计，也是较高级的联排式里弄住宅。由于与安乐邨同出一位建筑师之手，在建筑的空间构成及立面处理的手法方面有许多相同或相近之处。

疙瘩楼紧临河北路，虽为里弄住宅，但只有一幢，故并无弄道。总建筑面积1739平方米，由四个单元拼接而成，为四层砖木混合结构。各分户单元均有前后小院。庭院植有绿化，削弱所临街道的噪音，弥补了环境的不足。

疙瘩楼的立面处理非常有特色，外檐墙体为硫缸砖清水墙，一些砖面有凸出的“疙瘩”，形成特有的材质肌理美感，故称“疙瘩楼”。疙瘩楼具有浓郁的意大利建筑风格，比例和谐，形象生动，砌筑精美，材料质感与建筑的自然处理达到完美统一，堪称租界里弄住宅的精品。

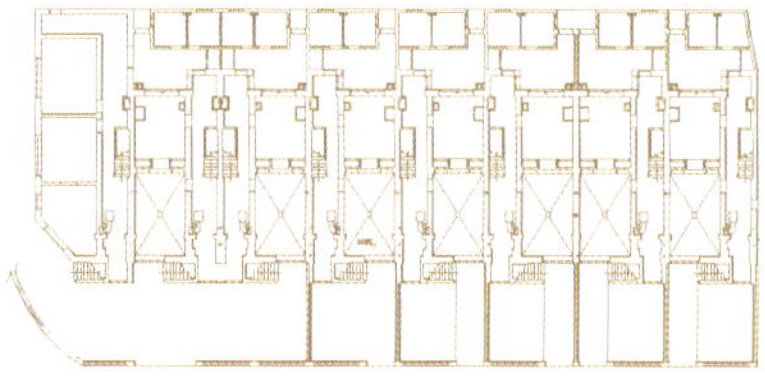
a. 首层平面图 Layout of the First Floor

b. 剖面图 Section Elevation

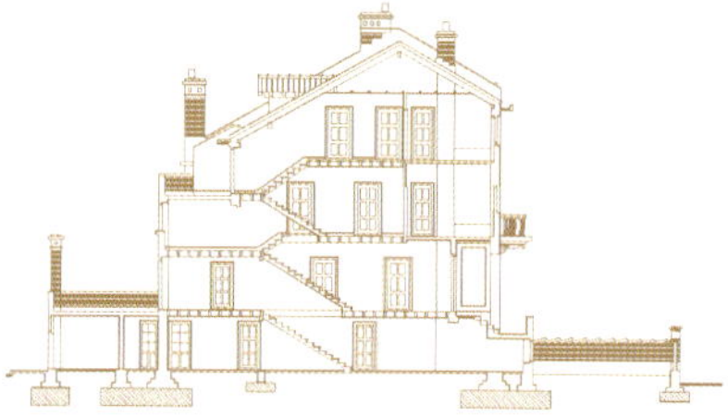
c. 立面图 Elevation

图7 疙瘩楼里弄住宅 Knotty Building Alleyway Residence

（五）集合式公寓住宅

集合式公寓住宅是二十世纪二三十年代出现的一种住宅类型，较传统住宅层数多，标准层户型有变化，以适用不同需要。起居、卧室、厨房、浴室、车库齐备，水、暖、电、卫设施齐全，标准较高，居住条件舒适。

1、民园大楼（图8）

民园大楼坐落在五大道地区，长沙路与重庆道交口处，建于1936—1937年，由奥地利建筑师盖苓（Rolf Geyling）设计。建筑总体平面大致为三角形，与地形相适应。砖混结构，地上四层，带半地下室。

公寓由四个单元组成，各单元均一梯两户，功能基本一致，但为适应朝向而调整户型组织手法。每户有起居室、卧室、厨房、备餐间和卫生间。

受现代建筑运动的影响，立面处理简洁朴实，自然得体。住宅外墙作水泥饰面，开窗基本一致，均为矩形窗。因其东立面较长，故划分为三段；两端以实墙面为主，对比强烈，界面规整。围墙以通透的方格形水泥构件拼砌，较有特色。

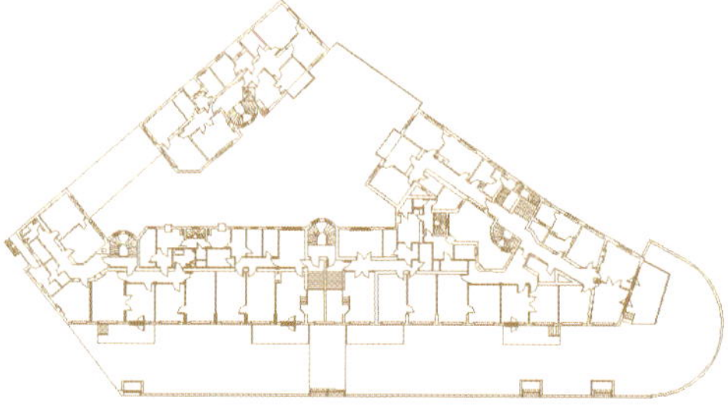
图8 民园大楼首层平面图
Fig.9 Layout of the First Floor of Min  of Min Yuan Building

2、利华大楼（图9）

利华大楼，属办公兼居住的公寓建筑，坐落在和平区解放北路114号，现为办公楼。该楼建于1936~1938年，由法籍永和工程公司（Brossard Mopin Tientsin Branch）设计施工，设计人为法国建筑师慕乐（P. Muller）。

二十世纪三十年代，受现代建筑运动影响，中国出现了一些造型简洁明快，表现材料质感的现代建筑。利华大楼就是天津在这一潮流影响下出现的最早几幢具有现代功能和技术的高层建筑之一。

建筑分主楼与东、西配楼，主、配楼共同围合成方形庭院。主楼十层，为钢筋混凝土框架结构，楼板多作现浇钢筋混凝土密肋板。建筑的功能分区明确，各楼层布局合理。首层为营业大厅，二至八层为高级公寓，以供出租，各公寓由过厅、客房、会客室、盥洗室、厨房及餐厅组成，设施一应俱全。利华大楼室内装修比较考究。主楼立面处理简洁生动，虚实对比强烈，材料质感丰富。外墙贴棕褐色麻面面砖，开窗较大，为通高大玻璃窗，钢质窗框。东南、西南转角部分均为弧形窗，线条舒展流畅，八层以上东、南两面逐层退进。整个建筑造型刚劲挺拔，体现了与传统建筑、“小洋楼”等迥异的现代建筑风格，是同时代高层建筑中的精品。

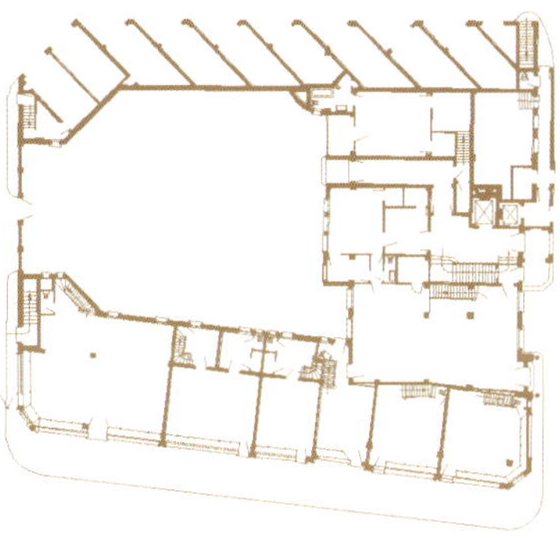

a. 首层平面图 Layout of the First Floor

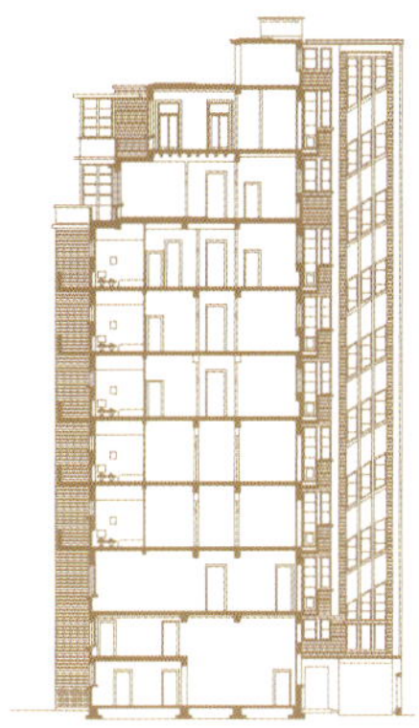

b. 剖面图 Section Elevation

图9 利华大楼 Leopold Building

# An Overview of Tianjin Historic Residential Buildings

Lu Hong[①] Zhao Jianbo[②]

Historic buildings refer to the legally protected historical buildings conforming to the Regulations on the Protection of Tianjin City's Historic and Stylistic Architecture. Currently there are 746 historic buildings approved by Tianjin Municipal Government, covering an area of 1.14 million square meters. Among them 560 are residential, accounting for 75%. They cover an area of 590,000 square meters, accounting for 52% of the total area. No matter in terms of quantity or type, residential buildings occupy an outstanding status. A great amount of residential buildings with proper size, beautiful appearance and harmonious color make up an important urban texture of Tianjin in modern history. They were also praised by Chairman Mao Zedong as one of the leading roles of "Beijing's quadrangles and Tianjin's western-style buildings". This paper is aimed to analyze Tianjin historic residential buildings in a comparative approach with detailed and accurate data so as to offer a systematic analysis and a perspective appreciation for those who are concerned with Tianjin historic buildings.

## I. Development

Of all the standing historic residential buildings, there are the Mansion of the Shi's Family and the Mansion of the Xu's Family built as early as in 1875 and the 1890s respectively; there is also Leopold Building built later in 1943. During nearly 70 years, Tianjin had undergone the changing of dynasties and the successive years of wars including the last years of the Qing Dynasty, the Beiyang Warlords, the nine concessions, Republic of China, War of Resistance against Japan and War of Liberation, which greatly affected the construction and development of residential buildings. This paper sums up it into four stages according to different characteristics.

### (I) The old city proper: traditional form of urban residence

Tianjin originated from the mouth of the old Sancha River, located at the convergence of the North Grand Canal, the South Grand Canal and the Haihe River. It benefited from navigation and water transportation in successive dynasties, so its economy grew promptly. Around Jin and Yuan Dynasties, Tianjin started to establish communities. In the second year of the Yongle Reign of the Ming Dynasty (the year of 1404), Tianjin set up garrison. In the third year of the Yongzheng Reign of the Qing Dynasty (the year of 1725), garrison changed into state. In the ninth year of the Yongzheng Reign (the year of 1731), state was elevated to prefecture. Tianjin became the imperial garrison and was growing into an important economic city in North China.

---

① Lu Hong, Director of the Specialist Consultative Committee Of Tianjin City Historic and Stylistic Constructions Protective Committee, doctor of engineering, senior architect.

② Zhao Jianbo, Associate professor of Tanjin University, School of Architecture, doctor of engineering.

In the Ming and Qing Dynasties, Tianjin was a typical city in North China plain. Covering an area of 1.76 kilo square meters, it is a walled rectangle with the Drum Tower as the center as well as roads crisscrossed. There used to be a saying: The rich lived at the north gate, the noble at the east gate, the poor at the south gate and the humble at the west gate. Government offices gathered to the north of the East-west Street while the residential area to the south of the East-west Street. The residences of the time were mostly traditional courtyard buildings of North China (such as the Mansion of the Xu's Family) and simple cottages. The population density was quite great. By the Daoguang Reign of the Qing Dynasty, the population reached 200,000, spreading from the old city to both banks of the mouth of the Sancha River.

In 1860, Tianjin was forced to open its port. At the very beginning, the old city proper maintained the prosperity with hundreds of merchants swarming. Even foreign merchants lived in the old city, and some of them placed their stores there. The four main roads were lined with alleys and lanes on both sides, and thus numerous communities formed. Except for a few government offices and the Confucian Temple that were traditional large-scale architecture, residences were mostly small-scale architecture mixed with partial residences of south China style. A blending of traditional Chinese architectural styles of both south and north was presented. On the gate tower and external walls of some residences, western architectural signs can be seen, which reflected the social trend of "the spread of Western influences to the East".

In 1900, the Eight-power Allied Forces invaded and occupied Tianjin. After breaking the city gate, they robbed in public for three days, and then set the city on fire. Such a calamity debilitated the old city. Afterwards, the Mutiny of 1912 as well as the two wars between the Zhili Warlords and the Manchurian Warlords brought the city in a state of devastation. The propertied class thought there was no safety for their lives and assets, so they moved to concessions for shelter in succession. The old city proper gradually became a civilian area or slum. The residential construction remained stagnant for many years. The old city was declining.

**(II) Concession: residential construction in the "state within a state"**

In 1860, the Second Opium War waged by the Anglo-French Allied Force made the Qing Government sign the Treaty of Beijing with Britain and France. As a result, Tianjin opened its port and became an open port; on December 7 of the same year, Britain established first concession in Tianjin followed by France, America, Germany, Japan, Russia, Belgium, Italy and Austro-Hungarian Empire. The concessions were constantly expanded. From the beginning till the final formation, the concessions were enlarged to cover an area of about 14 kilo square meters, eight times of the old city. Since the set-up of the first concession in 1860 to the extinction of the last in 1945, in as long as 85 years, imperialist powers established municipal councils in their own concessions one after another to construct those "states within a state" according to their own intentions. Due to the lack of unified and complete planning and Chinese's incapability to interfere into the affairs of concessions, dual characteristics of urban construction took shape: on the one hand, the city was a disorderly mixture; on the other hand, each concession was orderly planned with distinct features.

**1. Residential construction of French concession**

The French Concession (1860—1945) covered an area of 189 hectare. The main residential area was the community around the Quanyechang Mall and the Central Park next to the busy Middle Street (the present North Jiefang Road).

At first, the area of the Quanyechang Mall was an open space with pools and graves. The price of land was quite low. In 1900 when it was first developed as the French Concession, the appearance didn't change much. Along with the construction of the Middle Street, land jobbers realized the promising future of the area. Since then, land speculation became more and more flourishing; the price of land became several times of the original in sudden. The area turned into a magic weapon for land agents to acquire wealth. In the 1920s, the commerce of the area started to boom. A great many commercial and entertainment buildings such as stores, hotels, restaurants and cinemas were constructed, making the area a rising commercial center of Tianjin.

Meanwhile, residential buildings stood up around the area. After the Revolution of 1911, warlords, bureaucrats and new capitalists moved to live in the concession. They not only built luxurious residences (mostly detached residence) for their own enjoyment, but also rented new lanes and alleys to their employees for profits. Some compradors and new capitalists built residences on Xiafei Road (the present Huayuan Road) around the French Park (the present Central Park, see Fig. 1) while warlords built private residences on both sides of the Fenglingshi Road (the present Chifeng Road). At the peak time, there were a dozen of provincial military governors of the Republic of China living on Chifeng Road, which gave the road another name, "Governor Street". At that time, influenced by Shanghai Shikumen, the French Concession started to build new alleyway housing.

**2. Residential construction of British Concession**

As the earliest and biggest concession among the nine, the British Concession (1860—1943) covered an area of 410 hectare. The main residential area was the new area of British Concession (the present Fifth Avenue Area) and Taian Avenue.

In the 1880s, the Haihe River silted up gradually, which seriously affected the development of Tianjin navigation. The interests of concession countries were closely related to the smoothness of the Haihe River. Therefore, the Haihe River Engineering Bureau was founded in 1897 for the purpose of dredging and reforming the downstream waterways. During more than 20 years from 1902 to 1923, six times of dredging and desilting were performed. The river was cut off so that both upstream and downstream riverbeds were deepened and broadened, and then the waterways became smooth. Before 1927, a 2,000-tonner could sail to the urban area directly through the Haihe River. At the same time, the great amount of mud and silt dug out from each dredging were conveyed via iron pipes to low-lying swamps to fill and level them up, which was so-called "blowing mud for swamp filling".

The new area of the British Concession refers to the nearly 4,000 mu of land expanded outside Qiangzi River (the present Nanjing Road) by the British Concession in 1902. The area used to be low-lying swamp, and was improved in "blowing mud for swamp filling" at the beginning of this century, which enabled the spatial construction of the British Concession. From 1906 to 1928, the area was under municipal construction, including land preparation, road building, installing municipal facilities and some residential construction represented mainly by detached residence. Since the year of 1928, residential construction entered the period of community development, and the construction accelerated. Besides detached residence, new alleyway housing and assembled apartment were also in bloom. This area promptly became a high-class residential area. (see Fig. 2)

The new area of the British Concession was set up especially for constructing luxurious residence. In the 1920s, the theory of "garden city" planning was prevailing in Britain, so the planning and construction of the new area were very characteristic in accordance with the theory. For instance, the residential area was proper in scale, equipped with schools, churches, gardens and stadiums, thus a livable spatial scale and comfortable dwelling environment came into being. To ensure a good environment, no commercial center was established, moreover, trams and other public transportation vehicles were prohibited to enter. Therefore, the road scale in the area was quite small but pleasant. The new assembled apartment buildings, new alleyway housing and attached residences were transplanted to Tianjin directly from their birth places. Great importance was attached to land preparation and road building as well as complete municipal facilities such as road lamps, afforestation, water supply and sewerage. Additionally, flush toilets were introduced and promoted so that the living environment and the sanitation were improved. The western real estate development concept and mode were also introduced. The land was divided into four square parts enclosed by roads, thus facilitating the sale of the land by stages. It was strictly stipulated that in the British Concession, the buildings must be foreign-style; the scheme must be approved by the Municipal Council; however the residents were not limited to a certain nationality[①]. As a result, the variety of architectural styles in the residential area all had different ethnic features.

The superior dwelling environment of the new area attracted not only many bureaucrats, capitalists and retired politicians to build or rent their residences here, but also the middle and high classes previously living in the Hebei New Area and the area of Quanyechang Mall to move here. In a few years, the superior residential area of the Fifth Avenue Area including Machang Avenue, Munan Avenue, Dali Avenue, Changde Avenue and Chongqing Avenue took shape, which was the cluster of superior residential construction of Tianjin at that time.

**3. Residential construction of Italian Concession**

The Italian Concession (1902—1945) covered an area of 51.4 hectare. Besides barrack, consulate and the municipal council and other communal facilities, there were few commercial buildings but mostly residences (the present area of One-Palace Garden Area).

The Italian Concession had orderly and neat roads with fewer cinemas, theaters, opium dens and brothels. The tidy and peaceful environment attracted many retired warlords and frustrated politicians to build many villas here. They considered this treasure place a retreat away from the turmoil of the world. It explains why the buildings in the Italian Concession were mostly residential buildings represented by garden villas, such as the former residence of Liang Qichao built in 1914, Yingbingshi Studio built in 1924, the former residence of Tang Yulin, a Manchurian warlord, built in 1912 and the garden houses on Minzu Road. Besides superior detached housing, the Italian Concession also had new alleyway housing, such as the West Tuanjie Lane built in 1923 and the East Tuanjie Lane built in 1926.

Because the Municipal Council of the Italian Concession was very strict on architecture management, for example, it was stipulated that the facades of the buildings along the street should not be identical, so the existing buildings of the Italian Concession varied much in style. The appearance of the apartment buildings along the street were nice in particular while the visual quality of several main streets were distinct in style, especially the backbone roads including Minzu Road, Ziyou Avenue and Minsheng Road.

**4. Residential construction of Austro-Hungarian Concession**

The Austro-Hungarian Concession (1902—1917) covered an area of 68.7 hectare. The concession was constructed in quite a short period of time. It was constructed with an approach similar to the adjoining Italian Concession. The area next to the Haihe River was constructed mostly with public buildings in the earliest time, such as clubs and consulate, and later with residential buildings. After World War I, the Austro-Hungarian Empire returned the concession as a defeated country, but the residential construction continued. The still-existing residences include detached housing such as the former residence of the Yuan's Family and the former residence of Bao Guiqing as well as new alleyway housing such as the former residence of Feng Guozhang.

**5. Residential construction of German Concession**

The German Concession (1895—1917) covered an area of 280 hectare. It developed along the Haihe River and the South Jiefang Road. Besides dock warehouses, detached residences spread along the riverbank, in which people could enjoy the scenery of the river. On either side of South Jiefang Road were German Club, German Consulate and German Barrack. On the inner side of the road residential area was located. A mixed commercial and residential area with Xiaobailou Area as the center and a residential area

Note①: Yang Bingde.[M]// Modern Chinese Cities and Construction. Beijing: China Architecture & Building Press.1993,106.

around Fujian Road and Taiwan Road were formed. Besides detached housing, there were a lot of alleyway housing and enclosed housing, such as Zengyan Lane (see Fig. 3). The style and appearance of enclosed housing were obviously inherited from typical German residence.

**6. Residential construction of Japanese Concession**

Japanese Concession (1898—1943) covered an area of 143 hectare. With Xu Street (the present Heping Road) paralleling the Haihe River as the commercial center, the concession placed administrative, military organizations, schools and a few detached residences such as the Jingyuan Garden and the former residence of Mr. Zhang on Gongdao Street (the present Anshan Avenue) which was perpendicular to the Haihe River. Among the four sections formed by crisscrossed Xu Street and Gongdao Street, the two to the north of Xu Street along the Haihe River were commercial while the two to the south were residential with mostly new alleyway housing. Compared to the British, French, German and Italian concessions, the Japanese Concession's residential buildings were larger in scale but bad in quality and simple in single building. Oriental awareness could be found out in environment construction. Fewer historic buildings are preserved in the Japanese Concession.

**7. Residential construction of other concessions**

The Russian Concession (1900—1924) covered an area of 365 hectare. The concession was large, but due to its domestic turbulent political situation and a lack of funds, there was quite limited construction done in the concession. Now only the buildings of the consulate and the barrack are preserved, and part of residential buildings are preserved along the present Shisanjing Road and Xiaowangzhuang.

The American Concession (1860—1902) covered an area of 8.7 hectare. America had been letting Britain manage the concession and later sold it to Britain. The concession had mainly public buildings, such as the British Club, Investment Invitation Bureau and Talati House Hotel.

The Belgian Concession (1902-1931) covered an area of 49 hectare. It was basically used as dock warehousing.

**(III) Hebei New Area: the new opportunity for urban development**

At the end of the nineteenth century, after the Beijing-Manchuria railway was open to traffic, the previously built train station (the old dragon head station, the present Tianjin East Train Station) was surrounded by the Austro-Hungarian, Italian and Russian concessions. In order to compete with foreign powers in commercial transportation, the Qing Dynasty implemented a new policy and launched the project of Hebei New Area. In 1903, a new train station was constructed in Xinkai River, which is the present North Station, and meanwhile the section from the present Zhongshan Road to Xinkai River was exploited to be a new area. On the basis of completing the road system of the new area, factories were set up; schools were founded; government offices were built; and clubs were established. Covering an area of 6.534 kilo square meters, the area had been becoming a rising industrial and commercial center of Tianjin.

After the Revolution of 1911, Hebei New Area became the location of the Beiyang Warlord Government. Many brands of the business circle placed their plants in the area. As a result, the number of civil service workers, railway workers, industrial and commercial workers suddenly rose. The residential construction of the new area entered the flourishing stage since then. Some warlords, officers and merchants grasped the opportunity to purchase land, build houses and rent them for profits. The residential buildings of the time were mostly courtyard alleyway housing serving middle and low classes. In addition, there were also some shabby dormitories mainly for industrial workers pouring into the city, such as Beiyang Dormitories. The residences were managed by local Chinese real estate agents. After the year of 1928 when the Beiyang Warlord domination ended, Hebei New Area was declining. The prosperity of concessions and the emergence of new alleyway housing made the courtyard alleyway housing vanish.

The construction of Hebei New Area can be considered a competition of Chinese government as a rival against the imperialist powers. The achievements it made can't be ignored. But the internal conflicts of the Beiyang Warlords finally led to its failure.

**(IV) Development of Nanshi: marginal zone between concessions and old city**

Located to the south of the old city and the west of the Japanese Concession, Nanshi used to be a piece of deserted wasteland. In 1903, Japan named it "reserved residence" when they expanded their concession. Since the Chinese government lost control of it for a long term, it was known as "land under nobody's jurisdiction".

Along with the flourishing of Xu Street in the Japanese Concession (the present north section of Heping Road), the potential economic values of this marginal zone became more and more apparent. Realizing it, many rich and powerful people came for land purchase and real estate operation, such as Dongxing Company run by Li Chun, a Jiangsu warlord, Zhende Real Estate Company run by Chen Guangyuan, a Jiangxi warlord and Rongye Real Estate Company founded by Rong Yuan. At that time, besides continuing the construction of courtyard alleyway housing and shabby cottages, some early-stage alleyway residences of Shikumen style emerged in Nanshi which were called "lock-style residence colloquially".

## II. Basic characteristics

**(I) The residential constructions of different stages vary distinctively**

Tianjin residential buildings constructed before 1860 were mostly self-built unshared housing. The residential form was traditional quadrangle of North China merged with some architectural style of South China.

The development of Tianjin residential buildings in modern history can be roughly divided into two phases with the year of 1910 as the boundary. In the first phase, residential construction moved closely with the economic center while in the second phase, pursuing after livable environment, convenient and peaceful areas were preferred for large-scale community construction.

When Tianjin first opened its port, the old city continued the prosperity of the old days. Even the merchants coming from Britain, France and other countries lived in the old city for the convenience of trade. The residential form was traditional quadrangle. Although arched corridor residence of foreign style appeared, it vanished due to the climate difference. At the end of the nineteenth century when Hebei New Area rose rapidly, the economic and political center of the city moved there. A great amount of courtyard alleyway housing emerged timely. The new area became the cluster of residential construction. As the penetration of urban economy to the marginal zone, large-scale residential construction took place in Nanshi. Some real estate companies built and managed a group of lock-style alleyway apartment buildings. Catching up from behind, the Quanyechang Mall area turned into a golden commercial section. A great quantity of new alleyway housing were built in the neighborhood. At the same time, a small detached residence group was also built.

When economy was relatively stable, residential construction didn't wander with the attraction of commercial interests anymore, but stayed where it was convenient, quiet and prosperous. Therefore, in the new area of the British Concession and the Italian Concession residences were exploited for the purpose of a livable and comfortable environment. Focusing on warehousing and trade, the Russian, Austro-Hungarian, German and Belgian concessions had much less residential construction.

**(II) The residential mode changed along with the development of social economy**

As an important trading port in North China, Tianjin was greatly influenced by foreign cultures, and the economic structure switched fast from natural economy to commodity economy. Such a sudden change led to rapid transformation of architecture in all aspects. On the one hand, traditional residences engaged in reform to adapt to new demands; on the other hand, foreign life style and architectural mode were gradually imitated and accepted. The residential mode had undergone great changes along with social changes. Correspondingly, as a result, residential buildings changed in terms of architectural form, functions and construction method.

First, fast urbanization resulted in the high density of residential construction.

Tianjin was only a 17.6 kilo square meters small town when it first opened port, and grew into a commercial center of North China at high speed. During a short period of dozens of years, the population grew vigorously in the process of urbanization. To be compatible with the fast urbanization, residences of high volume ratio fitting the architectural technology level must be constantly explored. In addition, raising the residential volume ratio was also in conformity with real estate agents' pursuit after profits. Therefore, the courtyard alleyway housing deriving from traditional quadrangle evolved into lock-style apartment housing and then new alleyway housing which originated from western attached housing. Through adding stories to generally three, new alleyway housing acquired enough space and comfort. It became the type of residential form which was built in biggest quantity in Tianjin in modern history.

Second, the functional layout of residence adapted to the life style.

Since the traditional life style was impacted by modern life style in modern society, the spatial framework and functional structure changed correspondingly. Traditional quadrangle had very neat spatial framework. The rooms were partitioned into central room, wing rooms, south room and side rooms according to position, but their functions were not fixed. Influenced by foreign life style, rooms were partitioned into living room, sitting room, bedroom, kitchen, dining room and storeroom and later garage according to function. The function determination of rooms made the residential layout more complicated. The development from courtyard alleyway housing to lock-style apartment housing then to new alleyway housing and later to detached housing reflected the process of changes.

The process of life style changes also left some spatial patterns of transitional period in residences. Although the architectural form and composition of space were western, traditional life style was revealed in many aspects. Let's take detached housing as an example. The appearance and space composition of the former residence of Prince Qing are western, but an ancestral temple was built on the added third storey, meanwhile a Chinese-style garden was built. The former residence of Zhuang Lefeng in the French Concession has a Buddha worshipping hall arranged at the affiliated part. Moreover, outbuildings were built behind main buildings in lock-style apartment housing, new alleyway housing and detached housing for servants' dwelling. It was obviously influenced by the concept of ranking by social status in traditional Chinese culture and the space composition of traditional quadrangle.

Third, the commercialization of modern times led to the change of residential construction and operation mode.

Under the original economic mode, traditional residences were built by private dwellers, so the construction speed was quite slow. With the accelerated urban modernization, in Tianjin with concessions accounting for the main body of the city, the simple construction and operation mode didn't suit the demands of social development. For instance, in Hebei New Area, which is a new economic and political center, the big inflow of population needed a lot of residences to be completed in a short term, so the uniformed construction and operation by real estate agents emerged at the right time. Of course, the early real estate construction and operation were mainly controlled by warlords and bureaucrats. The involvement of merchants came later. The uniformed construction and operation by real estate agents worked faster than traditional mode, so it was more suitable for tract development and adapted to the social development of the time. It was later adopted in the construction of Nanshi, the Quanyechang Mall area and the new area of the British Concession.

**(III) More construction took place in concessions than in the old city**

Covering only an area of 1.76 kilo square meters, the old city had so dense residences that it didn't have much space for development. The exploitation of Hebei New Area provided potential for development to some extent, but the area covered only an area of 6.534 kilo square meters. Comparatively, the nine concessions covered an area of 14 kilo square meters, eight times of the old city. Such a large area had potentials not only for constructing industrial warehouses and a wide range of business district, but also for the development of residential construction.

In modern times, China had been in turmoil with ceaseless natural and man-made calamities. However, it was relatively more secure in concessions, and the residential construction there had never paused. In concessions, on the one hand, each concession country depended on favorable policies to provide protection of political and economic interests for those residing there by means of foreign laws; on the other hand, in order to build Tianjin into a center of foreign affairs in North China, they made investments in concessions and adopted a series of land policies and municipal administration measures. Such advantages were very attractive to propertied class who came here to do business, reside or engage in real estate trade. It was the investment of the propertied class that enabled the prompt development of concessions. Hence, the residential construction of concessions outmatched that of the old city in scale, speed and quality, which revealed the unbalance of urban residential development of Tianjin in modern history.

**III. Style characteristics of modern residential architecture**

**(I) Individual style characteristics**

Modern residential buildings predominated Tianjin historic buildings. With concessions serving as the headquarters, modern residential buildings have very distinct style characteristics. Their evolution can be divided into three periods. The first period is represented by the transition of traditional residence to modern residence; the middle period had eclectic and classic revival architecture as the mainstream; the last period was targeted to develop modern residence. The three periods had their own backgrounds and features.

In early days, residential buildings were mostly arched corridor style. "They are an imitation of the residential buildings of Hong Kong which however came from India. The buildings have spatial inner space with abundant furniture and are ideal for residence in summer, but in winter, they look cold." ① The indiscriminate imitation resulted in inapplicability because of the climate differences and was abandoned shortly after. The early courtyard alleyway housing and lock-style apartment housing borrowed the array mode of western attached housing on the basis of the framework and form of traditional residential buildings. They reflected national features in detailed decoration, and also absorbed exotic elements. There were only a few detached residences. Rich people stilled dwelled in traditional Chinese-style residences. Generally speaking, in this period, residences were experiencing the transition from traditional to modern. The communication and fusion of Chinese and western cultures were demonstrated in architecture.

In the 1920s and 1930s, the western eclecticism and classic revivalism were prevailing. The western impact enabled the architectural trend popular in Tianjin, such an imperial colony in the Far East. The national bourgeoisie rising after the Revolution

Note①: Yang Bingde.[M]// Modern Chinese Cities and Construction. Beijing: China Architecture & Building Press.1993,92.

of 1911 had their life style westernized, influenced by western ideology and culture. It was also mirrored in architecture, by seeking novelty, unconventionality and natural acceptance of architectural eclecticism and classic revivalism. The residences of the period mostly applied eclecticism and classic revivalism to appearance. For instance, the former residence of Tang Yulin in the Italian Concession is a typical Italian classic revival architecture; and people can see Baroque columns and patterns, cornices and brief metal railing on the appearance of the former residence of Sun Dianying in the British Concession. It was not limited to detached housing. The new alleyway housing also demonstrated it. For example, the Lumpy Building merged different styles by using local materials as well as decorations of classic signs. The eclectic and classic trend didn't restrain until the late 1930s when the modern architecture movement got involved.

In the late 1930s, modern architecture was acknowledged universally for its brief forms and practical functions. It surpassed its predecessors and started to take root in Tianjin and developed. Soon it was found in all kinds of residential buildings, including alleyway housing, such as Daxing Village and Guilin Lane, detached housing, such as the former residence of Wang Zhanyuan, and assembled apartment housing, such as Hong Kong Building, Min Yuan Building and Mao Gen Building. High-rise office and apartment buildings emerged in Tianjin in modern forms, such as Leopold Building. The emergence of a group of modern buildings added freshness to Tianjin. However, modern residences didn't acquire adequate development owing to the fact that the construction and stability of concessions were broken by the upgrade of wars.

In summary, Tianjin residential buildings of modern times were mainly eclectic and kind of blending. The owners put things from different regions and times on one residence out of their interests and desire for unconventionality. It was architects' job to mix and mingle different elements in a harmonious way. The former residence of Zhang Ruiting in the region of French Park served as an example. Mansart roofs and classic columns showed the style of French classic architecture while the semi-circle parlor at the entrance was covered with modern roof made of transparent glass. However, there was no sense of disharmony. Similar approach was taken while building the former residence of Zhang Xueming.

**(II) Group style characteristics**

During the later period of the development of Tianjin residential architecture in modern times, with the maturity of real estate business, residential construction became independent and didn't wander any more under the influence of economic and industrial prosperity. Large-scale communities were exploited in the later period. A new trend of community housing became one of the characteristics of Tianjin residential architecture in modern times.

Tianjin residential communities in modern history were mostly distributed in the tract and linear forms. The residences were assembled with distinct style and features. Well-preserved regions include the residential area of the Fifth Avenue Area, the residential area of the French Park and the residential area of the Italian Park. Of them, the residential area of the Fifth Avenue Area was the most complex. It was stipulated by the authority of the British Concession that only foreign-style residences could be built while traditional Chinese residences were prohibited. Hence, British, Italian, Spanish, eclectic, classic and modern emerged in the area one after another. On the contrary, the residential areas of the French Park and the Italian Park were comparatively standard with typical French-style and Italian-style residences respectively. The residences of linear distribution were assembled and had their features as well, such as Anshan Avenue in the Japanese Concession and Chifeng Avenue in the French Concession.

The residences in a few large regions became the regional landmarks while all these communities also became the landmarks of Tianjin with their distinctive features. Tianjin was given the title of "International Architecture Expo" because of these distinctive residences which contain the architectural forms of different styles and different regions.

## IV. Types and examples

The residential architecture in Tianjin historic buildings is rich in forms and styles. This paper is going to brief them in five categories according to living forms.

### (I) Traditional Chinese quadrangle

#### Mansion of the Shi's Family

Located in Yangliuqing Town of Xiqing District, the Mansion of the Shi's Family is a special protection historic building, and now a museum. The Shi's family was one of the "eight distinguished families" of Tianjin in the Qing Dynasty. The residence belonged to Shi Yuanshi, a descendant of the Shi's family. The group of typical quadrangles was built in 1875. With the arrow road as the axis, the group of quadrangles are divided into east part and west part. There are 10 independent quadrangles and three-section compounds, in total over 200 rooms, covering an area of about 6,000 square meters and the floor area of about 3,000 square meters. The theatrical stage in the courtyard is quite a big folk house theatrical stage in North China. The residence is brick-wood structure with flush gable roofs, lambdoidal ridges or ingot ridges, and black-bricked external walls. The brick, wood and stone sculptures are refined in technique and unique in profiling, and borrowed from western architectural decorations, so they have great visual value.

### (II) Western detached housing

Early in the twentieth century, detached housing was introduced to China. Since the 1920s, some big cities including Shanghai, Nanjing, Tianjin and Qingdao had their economy developing fast. Many foreigners, bureaucrats and capitalists living in the mentioned cities dwelled in detached residences, so this residential form became to prevail. As to Tianjin, although detached residence showed up as early as the period of the construction of Hebei New Area, the quantity was rather small. Until the end of the 1920s, detached housing gradually contributed to the look of western-style buildings of Tianjin in modern times.

The detached residences of Tianjin absorbed the western experiences in layout, form, technology and facility, and at the same time maintained the Chinese conventions in inner decoration and courtyard landscape engineering. The mixture of European technology and equipment, western residential style and traditional Chinese life style constituted a complicated compound. It reflected the life features and ideological characteristics of the upper class at that time. The residences tended to be novel, which reflected that the residents intended to show off their economic strength and boast their love of life. The residences comprised of main buildings and outbuildings which were behind the main ones. Of course it was the result of functional division, but it also expressed the hierarchical social structure. The center of the main space was always a big two-storied hall serving as public space for social intercourse, which also mirrored the fashion of western life style then.

#### 1. The Former Residence of Li Jifu (see Fig. 4)

Li Jifu was the comprador of Gibb Livingston & Co., one of the four foreign firms in Tianjin in modern times. His residence was the biggest high-class detached villa near the Central Park, located at 12 Huayuan Road in the French Concession. Built in 1918, the residence was designed by a Swiss Engineering Company and covers an area of 4,890 square meters.

Facing south, the residence is opposite to the Central Park. It is symmetric with a north-south axis. The main building is a brick-wood structure with one floor (partially two floors) on the ground and one floor underground. Three buildings form an isosceles triangle surrounding the square courtyard. Chinese-style outbuildings are placed at the northeast and northwest corners.

The courtyard is the center of the architectural space. All parts of the building are developed surrounding it and form a very beautiful environment. The east and west buildings to the courtyard have square architectural planes. They both have a square hall with a winding corridor in the middle as the center surrounded by bedroom, living room, dining room, pantry, study and washing room as well as a group of accessory rooms connected to it. The square hall running through the two stories is covered with a crossed arch. There are four semi-circle arched windows around the arch. The central courtyard and the square hall served as the main parts of the residence and made the composition of space unconventional, which is rather rare in so many detached residences in Tianjin in modern times. The architectural composition of the building is clear. It has red-bricked walls without plastering and partial exposed aggregate finish. The cornices and window cases are decorated with classic architrave.

**2. The Garden house on Minzu Road of the Italian Concession (see Fig.5)**

In traditional Italian cities, square is the most typical. Magnificent squares can be found in most Italian cities. Statues and monuments were erected as the visual center of a square. Even in the Italian Concession in Tianjin which is so far away from Italy, the tradition was still kept. A new-style Corinthian column stands in the center of the square in memory of Marco Polo. A statue stands on the top of the column. The base is decorated with sculptures. The column stands in a fountain.

From 1908 to 1916, eight detached residences had been constructed on the edge of the square one after another. Their layouts are largely identical with minor differences. Living room and sitting rooms are on the first floor. Bedrooms are on the second floor. The staircases lead to the balcony on the roof. The elevation adopted light-colored decorative finish. Ionic colonnade is set at the entrance. Cornices partially have tile hanging which naturally transits to parapet. A tower pavilion stands on the verge of the square. Sculptures decorate the lower part of eaves and the upper part of the openings in the wall.

Since it was required by the Municipal Council of the Italian Concession that the architectural form of the buildings in the concession should not be identical, the residences have uniform style, similar but not identical forms, even the tower pavilions vary. The square coexists with surrounding residences in harmony. Thus a typical Italian city view is reproduced.

**(III) Courtyard alleyway housing**

Originating from Tianjin, courtyard alleyway housing spread outwards with Tianjin as the center. It was influential in North China. As a main type of alleyway housing in Tianjin in the early stage, courtyard alleyway housing, influenced by western attached housing, was developed on the foundation of the spatial form of traditional three-section compounds of North China. It absorbed the dense layout of western attached housing, and adapted to the demands of social economy at that time. It was a flexible form of traditional quadrangle to adapt to the demand of commercialization and high density of residence.

**Tong Qing Lane (see Fig. 6)**

Located at the east side of the north end of Ancient Culture Street of Nankai District, Tong Qing Lane is an important protection historic architecture and commercial real estate now. Built at the end of the Qing Dynasty, it covers an area of 1,800 square meters with a floorage of 2,100 square meters. It is a lane constituted by 10 independent courtyards. There are bridge galleries at the entrance and exit of the lane, which creates a strong sense of spatial belonging. There are two two-storied black-brick buildings facing each other in each courtyard with brick-wood structures and sloping roofs. Open verandas are set on both stories. Traditional Chinese and western architectural elements can be found in architectural function, style, decoration and the layout of the lane. The residential styles of both North China and South China are combined while both oriental and western architectural symbols are gathered, which make the lane a representative of eclectic architecture in modern history of Tianjin.

**(IV) New alleyway housing**

At the beginning of the 1920s, new alleyway housing emerged in Tianjin. In the early stage, the buildings assembled in the Quanyechang Mall area of the French Concession, and some in the Italian Concession. After the exploitation of the new area of the British Concession, new alleyway housing was largely assembled there.

New alleyway residence normally had two or three stories, attached to each other and dwelled by a single household. According to size, units were divided into single room, one and a half rooms, two rooms, two and a half rooms and free layout. Among the five types, one-and-a-half-room residences were most built. There was a clear division of room functions in each unit. Living rooms, bedrooms, kitchens, washing rooms, garages and servant' rooms were reasonably distributed according to functional demand. Each unit had independent entrance and exit. The residence was normally brick-wood structure. A small amount of brick and concrete structure was adopted only in the later stage. It had complete facilities and plain inner decoration. New alleyway housing paid attention to the combination of building and environment. The courtyard and alley roads were beautifully afforested. The living environment was peaceful and comfortable. The small courtyard served as a transitional space. The space for sundries was set at the back of the residence. The residences in a block had styles of different western countries.

**1. Anle Village (see Fig.7)**

Anle Village is located near the crossing of Machang Avenue, Munan Avenue and Guilin Road. It is a high-class attached new alleyway residential lane, designed by P. Bonetti, an Italian architect in 1933. The residents were mostly middle and senior clerks.

It has three buildings laid in peripheral and row patterns. The alley paths in-between are wide. It has good sun exposure and ventilation. Each household unit has both forecourt and backyard. The forecourt is semi-open and afforested while the backyard is smaller. Trees are planted on both sides of the alley paths and in the forecourts, so the living environment is quite beautiful and comfortable.

**2. Knotty Building (see Fig.8)**

Built in 1937, Knotty Building is located at 283~295 Hebei Road. It is a high-class attached alleyway residence, designed by P. Bonetti, the Italian architect who also designed Anle Village, so same or similar composition of space and treatment of elevation can be found in the two.

Knotty Building is next to Hebei Road. Although it is an alleyway residence, there is only one building and no alley path. The total floorage is 1,739 square meters. It is a four-storied brick-wood structure with four units connecting to each other. Each household unit has both afforested forecourt and backyard so as to reduce the noises from the street and make up for the flaw of environment.

The elevation treatment of Knotty Building is quite unique. The external walls are quarry-tiled without plastering. Some of the bricks protrude with uneven knotty, and thus a sense of beauty is created by this special texture. That also explains how it got the name. The building reveals strong Italian architectural style with harmonious scale, vivid appearance, exquisite engineering, quality materials and natural treatment. It is one of the masterpieces of alleyway residences in concessions.

**(V) Assembled apartment housing**

Assembled apartment housing is a type of residence emerging in the 1920s and 1930s. It has more storeys than traditional residence and different internal layout to adapt to different needs. It is equipped with complete facilities including living rooms, bedrooms, kitchens, bathrooms, garage as well as water, heating, electricity and sanitary facilities, so the living conditions are high and comfortable.

**1. Min Yuan Building (see Fig.9)**

Min Yuan Building is located at the crossing of Changsha Road and Chongqing Avenue in the area of the Fifth Avenue Area. It was designed by Rolf Geyling, an Austrian architect, and built from 1936—1937. To suit the landform, the building is a triangle. A brick-concrete structure has four floors on the ground and a semi-basement.

The building has four units, each with a staircase and two households. Their functions are almost the same with slight adjustment of internal layout to adapt to orientation. Each household has a living room, bedrooms, a kitchen, a pantry and a washroom.

Influenced by modern architecture movement, the elevation treatment is simple and plain, but natural and proper. The external walls have cement finish. The windows are rectangular. Since the east elevation is long, it is divided into three sections. The two ends are brick walls. A strong contrast is created, and the interfaces are neat. The bounding walls are laid with hollow checker cement components, which is very characteristic.

**2. Leopold Building (see Fig.10)**

Leopold Building used to be an office and apartment building and now an office building, located at 114 North Jiefang Road of Heping District. It was designed and constructed by French Brossard Mopin Tientsin Branch in 1936—1938, and the designer was P. Muller, a French architect.

In the 1930s, impacted by modern architecture movement, some modern buildings with simple but vivid appearance and quality materials emerged in China. Leopold Building is one of the few earliest high rises with modern functions and technologies in Tianjin.

The building has a main building and two side buildings at the east and the west which enclose and form a square courtyard. The main building is a reinforced concrete frame structure with ten stories. The floor slab is cast-in-place reinforced concrete multi-ribbed plate. The building has a clear function division. Each floor is reasonably laid. The first floor is a business hall. From the second to eighth floors are high-class apartments for rent. Each apartment comprises of a gallery, a living room, a reception room, a washroom, a kitchen, a dining room and a complete set of facilities. The inner decoration is very exquisitely made. The elevation treatment of the main building is simple and vivid. It creates a strong sense of contrast, and the materials are rich in texture. The external walls are pasted with sepia pitted tiles. The windows are big glass windows with steel window frames. Curved windows with smooth lines are applied at the southeast and southwest corners. Above the eighth floor, the east and south sides retreat floor by floor. The building erects tall and straight. A modern architectural style which is totally different from traditional buildings or western-style buildings is displayed. It is a masterpiece of high rise of the time.

# Old City Area and the Other Area

# 老城厢及其他地区

# Mansion of the Shi's Family

# 石家大院

石家大院坐落于西青区杨柳青镇，全国重点文物保护单位，特殊保护等级历史风貌建筑，现为博物馆。石家为清代津门“八大家”之一，此宅系石家后人石元仕宅第。该建筑为典型的四合院住宅建筑群，始建于1875年。整个院落以“箭道”为中轴，分为东西两部分，共有十个独立的四合院或三合院，房屋二百余间，占地面积约6 000 $m^2$，建筑面积约3 000 $m^2$，院中的戏楼是我国北方规模较大的民居戏楼。房屋均为砖木结构，屋顶皆为硬山，起人字脊或元宝脊，外墙为青砖砌筑。砖、木、石雕等建筑装饰工艺精美，造型别致，并借鉴了西方建筑装饰特色，颇具观赏价值。

大门外景 Exterior view of the Main Gate

花园 Garden

The Mansion of the Shi's Family lies in the town of Yangliuqing, Xiqing District. It is listed as the important heritage site under state protection and the special protection historic architecture in Tianjin, and it is used as a museum now. The Shi's Family was one of the eight most celebrated Families in Tianjin in the Qing Dynasty. The resident introduced here belonged to Shi Yuanshi, one of the offspring of the Shi 's Family. Built in 1875, the Mansion was a complex design in the traditional Chinese courtyard house style—enclosing dwelling block with its inner courtyard. Taking the main passage as the axis, the buildings were arranged respectively on east and west sides along the passage. The Mansion consists of 10 blocks, some with buildings in four directions while some in three directions. There are more then 200 rooms in the Mansion. It covers an area of some 6,000 square meters and its floor area was about 3,000 square meters. Moreover, even a theater is located within the resident, which is considered as one of the larger scale theaters of the civil residents in North China. All the buildings are constructed with gables roofs, as well as the herringbone and curved ridges. The walls of the buildings are made of black brick, finished with exquisite carvings of brick, wood and stone. The design of the Mansion is merged with the Western architectural features, being more tasteful.

鸟瞰图 Bird's eye view

影壁 Screen wall

箭道 Main passage

院落 Courtyard

院落 Courtyard

内院门 Gateway to a courtyard

抱鼓石 Drum-shaped bearing stone

精美的木雕 Exquisite wood-carvings

内院门 Gateway to a courtyard

内院门 Gateway to a courtyard

内院门 Gateway to a courtyard

砖雕 Brick carving

砖雕 Brick carving

戏楼内景 Inner view of the Theater

柱础 Column base

戏楼内柱础 Column base in the Theater

内景 Inner view

# Former Residence of Xu Pu'an

# 徐朴庵旧宅

徐朴庵旧宅位于南开区老城厢东门里大街202号，天津市区、县文物保护单位，重点保护等级历史风貌建筑，俗称徐家大院，建于清末民初，现为老城博物馆。徐朴庵为英商麦加利银行买办。大院采用我国传统合院砖木结构体系，占地面积约1 400m$^2$，建筑面积约700m$^2$，建筑坐北朝南，中轴线由三进院落组成。东西两侧为箭道，是内部通道，可作紧急疏散用，具有天津地方特色。该建筑群均为中国传统民居小式做法，采用青瓦硬山屋顶，墙体采用青砖磨砖对缝，门窗为传统木雕和花饰。建筑中还装饰了大量做工精细、寓意吉祥的精美砖雕、木雕，堪称工艺杰作。

外檐局部 Partial outer-eaves

Located at 202 Inner Dong Men Street of Lao Cheng Xiang, Nankai District, the Former Residence of Xu Pu'an is the heritage site under city/county protection and the important protection historic architecture. Built in the end of Qing Dynasty, it used to be called Xu's Courtyard, and now is Old Town Museum. Xu Pu'an was a comprador of Chartered Bank of England. Covering an area of 1,400 square meters, the courtyard applied traditional Chinese brick-wood structure. With a floor area of 700 square meters, it faces south, the axis is constituted by three independent courtyards. On both east and west sides are arrow roads which are internal corridors used for emergency evacuation. It is of typical local feature. The groups of buildings are all traditional Chinese small-type residence including black-tile gable roof and grinding bricks jointing walls, doors and windows with wood carving and floral decoration. A great deal of fine brick sculptures and wooden sculptures with auspicious connotations and superior workmanship decorate the building, which is considered a masterwork of architecture.

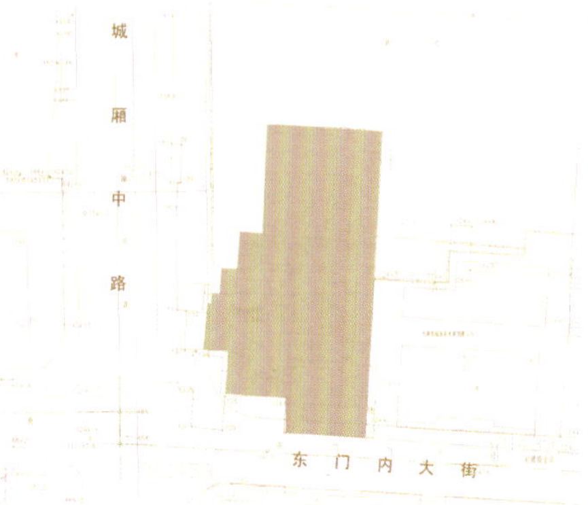

内院 Inner yard

↓影壁 Screen wall

内景 Inner view

↓馆内展品 Item on display in the yard

婚俗展示 Wedding customs show

# Tong Qing Lane
# 通庆里

通庆里位于南开区古文化街北端东侧，重点保护等级历史风貌建筑，现为商业用房。通庆里建于清末民初，占地面积约1 800 m$^2$，建筑面积约2 100 m$^2$，为六个独立的院落串联组成的里巷。建筑在里巷出入口处建有过街楼，具有较强的空间归属感。每个院落内相对有两座青砖二层楼房，砖木结构，坡屋顶，首层及二层均建有开敞外廊。建筑功能、风格、装饰和里巷布局既有中国传统建筑元素，又有西洋建筑符号，融合了中国南北方民居的风格，集萃了东西方建筑符号，是天津近代折中主义建筑的代表。

立面渲染图 Facade Rendering

Located at the east side of the north end of Ancient Culture Street of Nankai District, Tong Qing Lane is an important protection historic architecture and commercial real estate now. Built in the end of Qing Dynasty, it covers an area of 1,800 square meters with a floor area of 2,100 square meters. It is a lane constituted by six independent courtyards. There are bridge galleries at the entrance and exit of the lane, which creates a strong sense of spatial belonging. There are two two-storied black-brick buildings facing each other in each courtyard, which have a brick-wood structure and sloping roofs. Open verandas are set on both stories. Traditional Chinese and western architectural elements can be found out in architectural function, style, decorations and the layout of the lane. The residential styles of both north China and south China are combined while both oriental and western architectural symbols are gathered, which make the lane a representative of eclectic architecture in modern history of Tianjin.

内院 Inner yard

外景 Exterior view

通慶里
盛装开街
游客服务中心

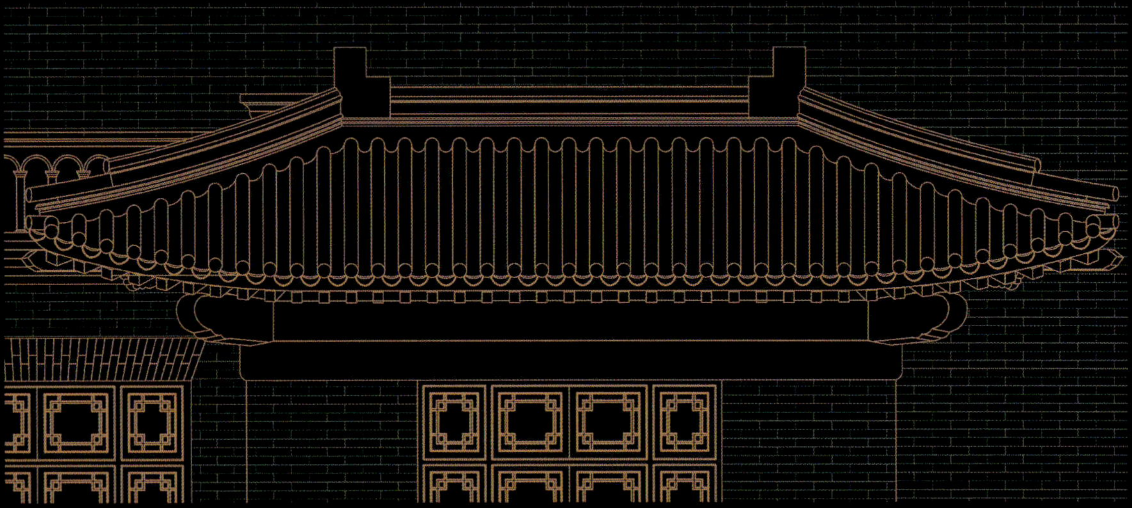

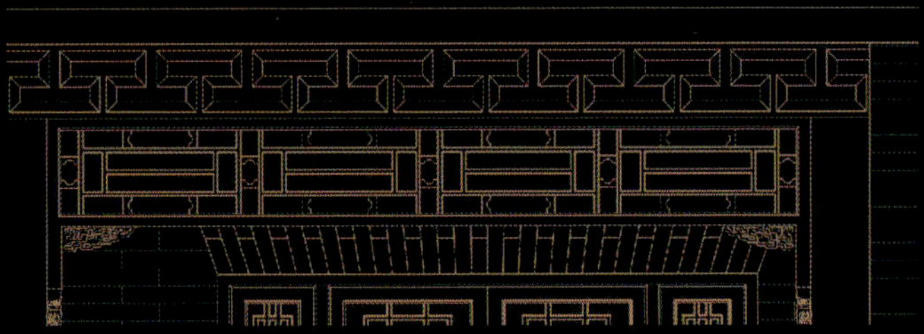

夜景 Night view

# The Residential Court of the Bian's Family at the Lane of Shen's Family Fence

## 沈家栅栏胡同卞家大院

沈家栅栏胡同卞家大院位于南开区鼓楼北街15号增1号。卞家为二十世纪初天津城里新“八大家”之首。卞家祖籍江苏省常州，清康熙五十四年（1715年）移居天津。至嘉庆八年（1803年），第四代“礼”字辈兄弟，开设了“隆顺号”，经营土产杂货，后又开设“隆顺榕”药店等企业，由此走向兴旺发达。至咸丰十年（1860）天津开埠之前，卞家已经成为天津巨富。1915年前后，卞家析产分家。

沈家栅栏胡同卞家大院为卞家第七代卞继昌析产后，在沈家栅栏胡同置地修建的宅院。该建筑为砖木结构平房形成的建筑群，规模虽小，建筑工艺却十分考究，至今仍保留着大量彩绘、砖雕、木雕。为典型的合院式建筑。

内院 Inner yard

外檐局部 Partial outer-eaves

The Residential Court of the Bian's Family is located at 15-1 of North Drum Tower Street Nankai District. The Bian's Family topped the new "eight illustrious families" of Tianjin in the early twentieth century. With the ancestral origin in Changzhou, Jiangsu Province, the Bian's Family moved to Tianjin in the 54th year of the reign of Kangxi of the Qing Dynasty (the year of 1715). By the eighth year of the reign of Jiaqing of the Qing Dynasty (the year of 1803), the fourth generation of the Bian's Family who had the first character of their given names as "Li" meaning propriety started a business dealing in local products and groceries named "Longshun", and later opened a pharmacy named "Longshunrong" and other businesses, which led the family to a road to prosperity. The family had already become a tycoon in Tianjin by the tenth year of the reign of Xianfeng of the Qing Dynasty (the year of 1860) when Tianjin opened its port. Around the year of 1915, the Bian's family split up and set up separate households.

砖雕 Brick carving

The Residential Court of the Bian's Family was built at the Lane of Shen's Family Fence by Bian Jichang, one of the seventh generation after the break-up of the family. It is a group of one-storied brick-wood structures. Although small in scale, the buildings are superior in architectural craftsmanship. Until now, a great deal of colored drawings, brick carvings and wood carvings are preserved. It is a typical enclosed court-style building.

内院门 Gateway to a courtyard

外景 Exterior view

砖雕 Brick carving

砖雕 Brick carving

外景 Exterior view

# Former Residence of Huo Yuanjia

# 霍元甲故居

霍元甲故居位于西青区小南河村，天津市文物保护单位，重点保护等级历史风貌建筑。霍元甲（1869—1909），字俊卿，天津人，出身武术世家。其父霍恩第是“秘踪拳”第六世传人。霍元甲自幼习武，尽得“秘踪拳”精髓，将“秘踪拳”发展为“迷踪艺”，开创了一代武林新风。1901年，俄国“大力士”来津演技，目空一切，出言侮辱中华，霍元甲挺身而出，将其击败，轰动津门。1909年他再次在上海击败英国“大力士”奥皮音，扬名沪上。同年霍元甲在上海闸北创立“中国精武体操会”，后改名“精武体育会”。是年9月，霍元甲因遭日本人毒害逝世。随后，其子霍东阁赴上海接办精武体育会，将中华武术发扬光大，并传播到了东南亚各国。1919年，孙中山先生曾为上海精武会题词“尚武精神”。

霍元甲故居约建于清咸丰年间，1988年在原址进行复原重修，为中国北方传统民居的三合院建筑，北房三间，东西厢房各一间。屋顶布青瓦，硬山小式结构，东南设门。建筑形制简朴，外观朴素。现为霍元甲纪念馆。

内院 Inner yard

影壁 Screen wall

Located at Xiao Nan He Village of Xiqing District, the Former Residence of Huo Yuanjia is the heritage site under city protection and the important protection historic architecture. Huo Yuanjia 1869—1909 with a coutesy name Junqing, was born in Tianjin. He came from a martial art family. His father, Huo Endi, was one of the sixth generation of descendents of Maze Boxing. Huo Yuanjia practised martial arts since he was very young, learned the essence of Maze Boxing and developed the boxing into an art and thus initiated a new age for martial arts. In 1901, a Russian man of muscle came to Tianjin to perform. He was arrogant and insulted Chinese people. Huo Yuanjia presented himself and beat the Russian up, which caused a sensation in Tianjin. He beat an strong English man in Shanghai in 1909 and became famous in Shanghai. He established China Jingwu Martial Arts Association in Zhabei, Shanghai in the same year, whose name was changed to Jingwu Sports Association. In September, Huo Yuanjia was poisoned by Japanese people and died. Later, his son, Huo Dongge, went to Shanghai and took over Jingwu Sports Association. He carried forward Chinese martial arts and spread them to all countries in Southeast Asia. In 1919, Sun Yat-sen ever wrote an inscription for Shanghai Jingwu Association, "Martial Spirit".

The former residence of Huo Yuanjia was built in Xianfeng Emperor's reign of Qing Dynasty and was renovated in 1988. It is a three-section compound of traditional residence of North China with three rooms on the north, one wing-room on the east and one on the west. It has black-tile roofs, small-type gable structure and gates on the southeast. The building has a plain and simple appearance. It is now Huo Yuanjia Memorial.

大门 Gate

内景 Inner view

内景 Inner view

# Former Residence of Qiao's Family

# 乔氏旧宅

乔氏旧宅位于和平区赤峰道70号，天津市区、县文物保护单位，重点保护等级历史风貌建筑，现为办公用房。乔氏为山西祁县人，祖宅即“乔家大院”。1875年，乔家设立忆中恒钱庄天津分号；1884年，设立大德通票号天津分号；1887年，设立大德恒票号天津分号。

乔氏旧宅为1917年乔家自建的建筑，位于原法租界，首层曾作为大德通票号使用，二楼用于居住。乔家掌门人乔映霞及其子乔铁汉、乔铁民曾在此居住。该建筑占地面积约1 700m$^2$，建筑面积约1 100m$^2$，由法国建筑师设计，砖木结构，坡屋顶，混水墙面。建筑立面采用对称构图，檐部中央设半圆形山花装饰，入口两侧为四组双柱承托的通敞外廊，水泥宝瓶镂空护栏，券式门窗点缀其间。建筑造型稳重大方，具有折中主义建筑特征。

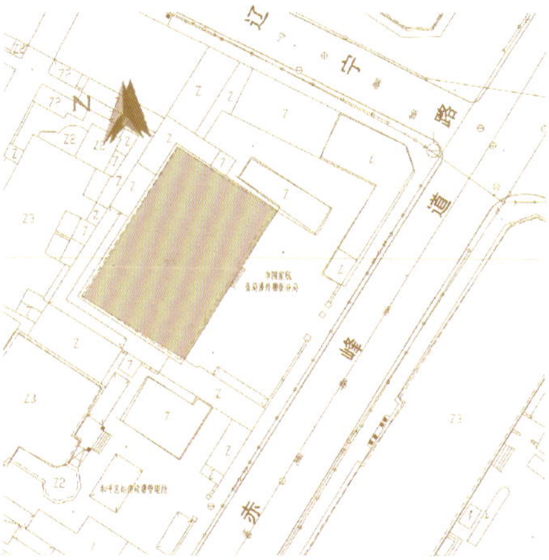


正立面渲染图 Facade Rendering

外景 Exterior view

外景 Exterior view

外檐走廊 Corridor of the outer-eaves

外檐门 Gate under the outer-eaves

内檐局部 Partial under the inner-eaves

Located at 70 Chifeng Avenue, Heping District, the Former Residence of Qiao's family is the heritage site under city/county protection and the important protection historic architecture and is now an office building. The Qiao's Family came from Qi County of Shanxi Province, the ancestral residence being "Qiao's Compound". The Qiao's family established Tianjin Branch of Yizhongheng Native Bank in 1875, the Tianjin Branch of Dadetong Native Bank in 1884 and the Tianjin Branch of Dadeheng Native Bank in 1887.

Located in the French concession, the Former Residence of Qiao's Family is a construction built by the Qiao's Family in 1917, the first floor being Dadetong Native Bank and the second floor for living. Qiao Yingxia, leader of the Qiao's Family, lived here with his sons Qiao Tiehan and Qiao Tiemin. Designed by a French architect, the two-storied brick-timber building with sloping roofs and plastered bricks walls covers an area of about 1,700 square meters and a floor area of about 1,100 square meters. The building facade adopted symmetric composition. The middle of the eaves is decorated with semicircular pediment; the open porticos supported by four groups of double columns are located at both sides of the entrance; hollow-out carved cement bottle guardrails, arch doors and windows are applied for decoration. The architectural modeling shows civility and elegance with a feature of eclecticism.

楼梯间内景 Inner view of staircase

内檐局部 Partial under the inner-eaves

# Former Residence of Fan Zhuzhai

## 范竹斋旧宅

外景 Exterior view

范竹斋旧宅位于和平区赤峰道76号，天津市区、县文物保护单位，重点保护等级历史风貌建筑，现为办公用房。范竹斋（1869—1949），名安荣，天津人。著名纱布商，天津“纱布业八大家”之一。1897年他任景德和棉纱庄驻沪主管，后升任经理；1932年成为东方汇理银行第五任华账房经理。范竹斋同时也投资房地产业，在天津法租界梨栈大街、城内鼓楼附近购置土地，建有竹远里、大安里、大庆里等处房屋。

该建筑占地面积约1 800 $m^2$，建筑面积约3 500 $m^2$，混合结构二层平顶楼房（带地下室），局部三层，混水墙面。建筑平面呈围合形式，首层、二层均设有外廊，其中首层为拱券式开敞通廊，顶部设有精美圆形角亭。建筑整体围合感很强，形成了宽敞的内部庭院。建筑外檐开窗较多，窗间饰以简化的西洋柱式和宝瓶等装饰，线条挺拔，立面丰富。该建筑具有典型的折中主义建筑特征。

立面渲染图 Facade Rendering

Located at 76 Chifeng Avenue of Heping District, the Former Residence of Fan Zhuzhai is the heritage site under city/county protection and the important protection historic architecture, and now an office building. Fan Zhuzhai, 1869—1949, with a coutesy name Anrong, was born in Tianjin. He is a famous businessman of cotton gauze and one of the eight great businessmen of cotton gauze in Tianjin as well. In 1897, he was the director of Jing De He Cotton Gauze Shop in Shanghai and later promoted as the manager. In 1932, he became the fifth Chinese director of the cashier's office of *Banque de l'Indo Chine*. He also invested in real estate business, purchased land in Lizhan Street of French concession and around the Drum Tower, and built Zhu Yuan Lane, Da An Lane and Da Qing Lane.

The Former Residence of Fan Zhuzhai covers an area of 1,800 square meters and a floor area of 3,500 square meters.

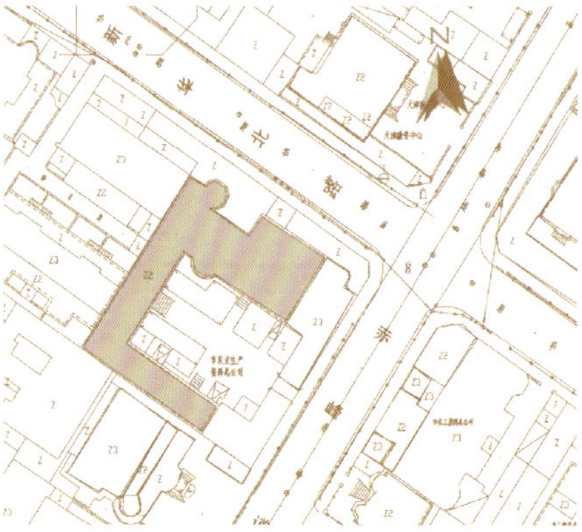

It is a two-storied flat-roofed mixed structure with a basement. It is partially three-storied with plastered brick walls. The construction plan is enclosed. Both storeys have verandas. The ones on the first floor are arch-type open verandas. On the top of the building is a fancy round corner pavilion. The whole architecture is a capacious courtyard, which has a strong sense of enclosure. On the external walls are many windows decorated with simplified western columns and goblets of forceful lines and rich facades. The architecture is a typical representative of eclectic architecture.

圆形角亭 Round corner pavilion

外檐局部 Partial outer-eaves

采光穹顶 Lighting Dome

外檐局部 Partial outer-eaves

壁炉 Fireplace

壁炉 Fireplace

老家具 Old-fashioned furniture

楼梯 Stairs

楼梯间 Staircase

# Former Residence of Chen Zhuling

# 陈祝龄旧宅

陈祝龄旧宅位于和平区保定道4号，重点保护等级历史风貌建筑，现为办公用房。陈祝龄，广东高要人，早年毕业于天津中西学堂，1880年经其堂兄介绍任天津怡和洋行大写，于1890年被委任为天津怡和洋行副买办。陈祝龄曾参股兴建了耀华里，并自己出资建造了大量房产，后组建义德洋行。

旧宅占地面积约1 300m$^2$，建筑面积约2 400m$^2$，混合结构三层楼房，局部二层，红瓦坡屋顶，外檐为清水红砖墙，门窗洞口多为拱券形式，同时设置精美的花饰、窗门套。建筑平面呈“L”形，造型美观典雅，体量错落有致，虚实对比强烈，并有较为宽敞的院落，具有折中主义建筑特征。

正立面渲染图 Facade Rendering

Located at 4 Baoding Avenue of Heping District, the Former Residence of Chen Zhuling is an important protection historic architecture, and now an office building. Chen Zhuling, born in Gaoyao, Guangdong Province, graduated from Tianjin Western School. In 1880, introduced by his cousin, Chen Zhuling worked in Tianjin Jardine Matheson, and was promoted as the vice comprador in 1890. Chen used to invest in building Yao Hua Lane, and built many houses on his own funds. Later he established Yoshinori Matheson.

The Former Residence of Chen Zhuling covers an area of 1,300 square meters and a floor area of 2,400 square meters. It is a three-storied and partially two-storied mixed structure with red-tile sloping roofs. The external walls are built with red bricks. The doors and windows are almost all arched with beautiful floral decoration and door and window frames. The whole building plane is in an "L" shape, pleasing and elegant. The comparison of abstractness and solidness of the building is strong. The capacious courtyard has the characteristics of eclectic architecture.

外景 Exterior view

会议室 Meeting room

↓内檐门 Gate under the inner-eaves

↓内景 Inner view

壁炉 Fireplace

↓老家具 Old-fashioned furniture

↓老穿衣镜 Old-fashioned mirror

老暖气片 Old-fashioned heating devices

木雕护墙板 Wooden wall-panels

老穿衣镜 Old-fashioned mirror

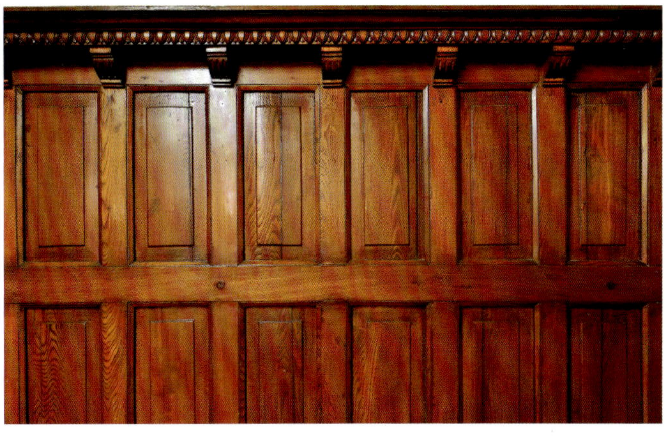

楼梯 Stairs

楼梯 Stairs

楼梯间 Staircase

楼梯间 Staircase

# Former Residence of Wu Chongxi

# 吴重熹旧宅

吴重熹旧宅位于和平区烟台道56~58号，一般保护等级历史风貌建筑，现为居住用房。吴重熹（1841—1921），山东无棣人，同治年间举人，曾任陈州知府、署理江西巡抚、河南巡抚、邮传侍郎等职。民国时期，他曾任袁世凯的名誉顾问，收藏金石、字画颇丰。

该建筑建于1912年，占地面积约1 600 m$^2$，建筑面积约1 200 m$^2$，砖木结构二层楼房，带地下室，青砖清水墙面，局部混水。多坡瓦屋顶，出老虎窗。建筑立面左右对称，两个主入口为条石高台阶，以柱承托突出局部三层，具有较强的导引性，屋顶间显示了木屋架特征。门窗均为木质，门窗套和外檐多处装饰精美得当。

外景 Exterior view

正立面渲染图 Facade Rendering

Located at 56~58 Yantai Avenue of Heping District, the Former Residence of Wu Chongxi is a general protection historic architecture, and now residential. Wu Chongxi 1841—1921 born in Wudi of Shangdong Province, was a provincial graduate in Tongzhi Emperor's reign of Qing Dynasty. He used to be the prefect of State Chen, the acting governor of Jiangxi Province, the governor of Henan Province and the assistant minister of mail communication. During the period of the Republic of China, he was the nominal consultant of Yuan Shikai, and collected a great deal of gold, precious stones, calligraphy and painting works. His former residence was built in 1912, covering an area of 1,600 square meters and a floor area of 1,200 square meters. It is a two-storied brick-wood structure with a basement. The outer-eaves are black-brick fair-faced walls and partially plastered. It has a multi-slope tiled roof and dormant windows. The elevation of the building is bilaterally symmetrical. The two main entrances are bar-stoned high steps. The partial three stories stand out with columns, which have a strong sense of guidance. Between the roofs are wooden roof trusses. Both doors and windows are wooden with beautiful decorations on door frames, window frames and external walls.

地砖 Tiles

外檐局部 Partial outer-eaves

↓外景 Exterior view

主入口 Main entrance

# Former Residence of Sun Chuanfang

# 孙传芳旧宅

孙传芳旧宅位于和平区泰安道17号，天津市文物保护单位，重点保护等级历史风貌建筑，现为办公用房。孙传芳（1885—1935），山东泰安人，毕业于北洋陆军速成学堂及日本士官学校，经廷试授步兵科举人。孙传芳最初在北洋军中任教官，辛亥革命后，曾任长江上游警备总司令兼第二师师长、福建军务督理、闽浙巡阅使兼浙江军务督理、五省联军总司令等职。北伐战争中他投靠奉系，被委为安国军第一军团长，与北伐军作战失利后寓居天津，与靳云鹏创办居士林，以诵佛经度日，并购置房产多处。1935年在居士林，被为父报仇的施剑翘击毙。

该建筑建于1922年，占地面积约5 200m$^2$，建筑面积约2 400m$^2$，由华信工程司建筑师沈理源设计。此楼原为北洋政府财政总长张弧住宅，1925年曾作为日本便衣队的情报传递点，1933年孙传芳购得此房。该建筑为混合结构二层楼房，红瓦坡顶配设造型独特的牛眼窗，混水墙面。一、二层均设回廊，正立面入口门廊由四根爱奥尼克柱式支撑山花。造型简洁大方，具有西洋古典主义建筑特征。

外景 Exterior view

正立面渲染图 Facade Rendering

左侧立面渲染图 Rendering of the left-side elevation

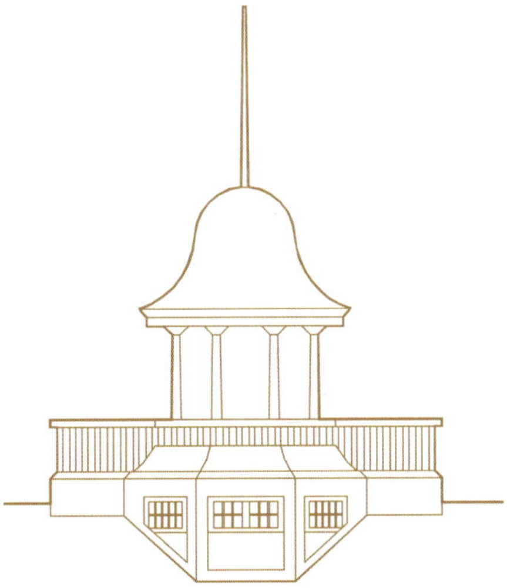

Located at 17 Tai'an Avenue, Heping District, the Former Residence of Sun Chuanfang is the heritage site under city protection and the important protection historic architecture and is now an office building. Sun Chuanfang (1885–1935) was born in Tai'an, Shandong Province. Graduating from Beiyang Land Force Fast-paced Academy and Imperial Japanese Army Academy, he was a successful candidate in the imperial examinations at the provincial level of infantry category after the final imperial examination. At first, he taught at Beiyang Army. After the Revolution of 1911, he was appointed garrison commander-in-chief at upstream of the Yangtze River and the commander of the Second Division, superintendent of the military affairs in Fujian, inspector of Fujian and Zhejiang and superintendent of the military affairs in Zhejiang as well as commander-in-chief of provincial allied forces etc. During the Northern Expedition War, he threw himself into the lap of the Feng Xi and was named regiment commander of the First Army Corps of Anguo Army. He lived in Tianjin after being defeated by the Northern Expedition Army, founding Jushilin with Jin Yunpeng and spending his time in reading Buddhist sutras. He also purchased many houses. In 1935, he was shot to death in Jushilin by Shi Jianqiao, who revenged for his father.

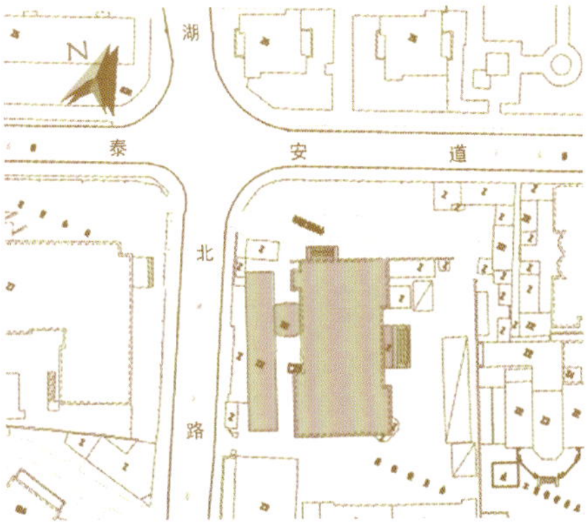


Designed by Shen Liyuan, an architect of Engineering Department of Huaxin, the building was constructed in 1922, covering an area of about 5,200 square meters and a floor area of about 2,400 square meters. It was formerly a residence of Zhang Hu, financial minister of the Beiyang government. The Japanese plainclothes policemen had took it as an intelligence transmission point in 1925 and Sun Chuanfang purchased it in 1933. The building is a two-storied building in mixed structure, with red-tiled sloping roofs installed with shed dormers in unique modeling and plastered brick walls. Cloisters were built in the first and the second floor. Four Ionic columns support the pediment at the main entrance porch. The architectural modeling is concise and elegant with a feature of western classicalism.

背立面 Back elevation

雪景 Snow view

外檐局部 Partial outer-eaves

侧入口 Side entrance

↓外檐门 Gate under the outer-eaves

↓外檐窗Windows below the outer-eaves

二层走廊 Corridor on the second floor

楼梯间内景 Inner view of staircase

↓壁炉 Fireplace

天花板 Ceiling

↓地砖 Tiles

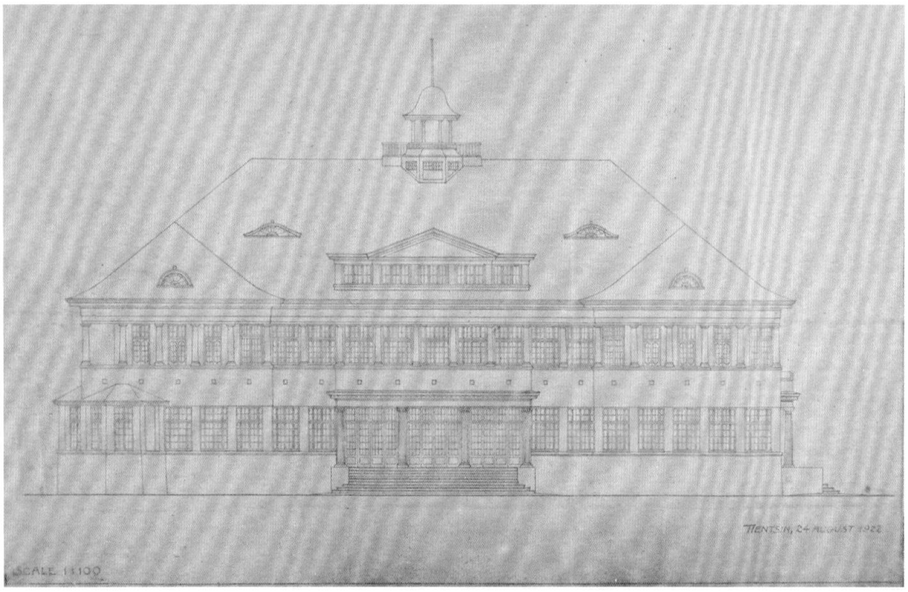


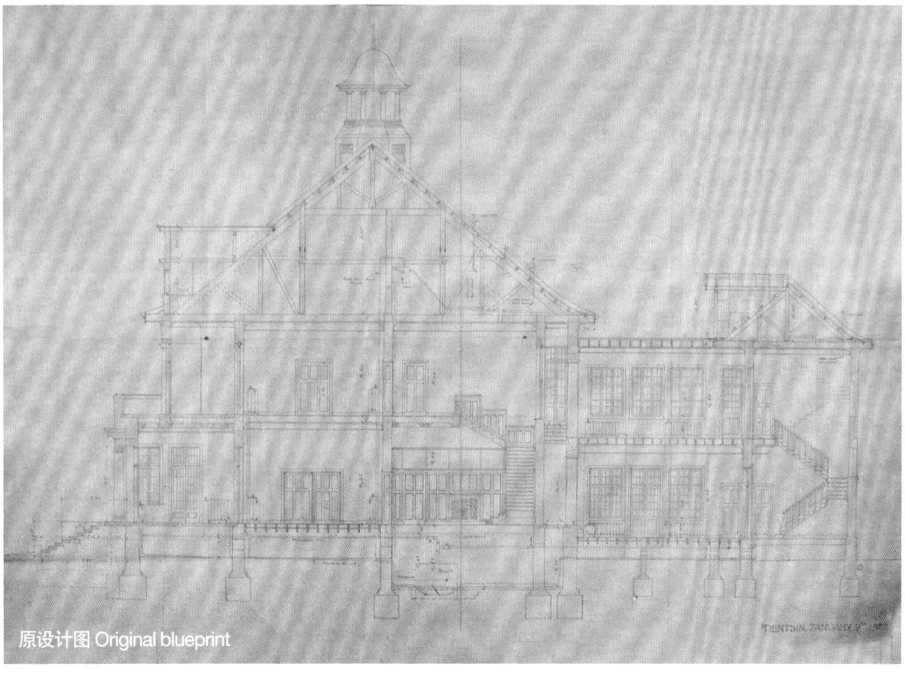

原设计图 Original blueprint

老暖气罩 Old-fashioned radiator enclosure

室内装饰 Decoration under the inner-eaves

# Former Residence of Sun's Family

# 元隆孙旧宅

元隆孙旧宅位于和平区新华路120号，天津市文物保护单位，重点保护等级历史风貌建筑，现为办公用房。“元隆孙”系指元隆绸布店创始者与经营者孙氏家族，代表人物为孙烺轩及孙仲凯父子。孙烺轩（？—1921），天津人，原为益泰昌布店学徒，后升任经理，1896年与人合资开设元隆绸布店，1915年又合资开办晋丰银号、元裕及元聚纱布庄，死后由次子孙仲凯接任。孙仲凯（1898—1966），名祥琪，原在银号学徒，1921年接任元隆绸布店经理，开办庆生棉纱庄，包销裕元纱厂棉纱，同时投资其他棉纱庄以及银号、米面庄等，后在劝业场和小白楼增设“元隆”新店，是民国天津商界“新八大家”之一。

旧宅建于1933年，由孙仲凯及其族人居住。该建筑占地面积约3 100m$^2$，建筑面积约3 000m$^2$，由中国工程司建筑师阎子亨设计，为砖混结构二层楼房，多坡屋顶，清水砖墙。建筑整体感较强，具有古典主义建筑特征。

正立面渲染图 Facade Rendering

Located at 120 Xinhua Road, Heping District, the Former Residence of Sun's Family is the heritage site under city protection and the important protection historic architecture and is now an office building. “Yuanlong Sun” refers to the founder of Yuanlong Silk Fabrics Store and the operator of the Sun's Family, represented by Sun Langxuan and Sun Zhongkai, i.e. father and son. Sun Langxuan (?–1921) was born in Tianjin, formerly an apprentice in Yitaichang drapery store and later promoted to manager. In 1896, he jointly ventured the Yuanlong Silk Fabric Store and also the Jinfeng Native Bank in 1915 as well as Yuanyu and Yuanju Gauze Store. His second son Sun Zhongkai succeeded him after his death. Sun Zhongkai (1898–1966), named Xiangqi, apprenticed in the native bank initially and took the position of Yuanlong Silk Fabric Store in 1921. He founded Qingsheng Cotton Yarn Store to underwrite the cotton yarn of Yuyuan Cotton Mill. Meanwhile he invested in other cotton yarn stores, native banks, rice and flour stores etc. Later he set up new “Yuanlong” stores in Quanyechang Mall and Xiaobailou. He was one of the “Eight New Distinguished Families” in Tianjin business circle during the period of the Republic of China.

The house was built in 1933, resided by Sun Zhongkai and his family members. It covers an area of about 3,100 square meters and a floor area of about 3,000 square meters. Designed by Yan Ziheng, an architect of Chinese Engineering Unit, the building is in brick masonry structure and has two stories, with multiple sloping roofs and fair-faced walls. The building has a strong sense of wholeness and also a classical architectural feature.

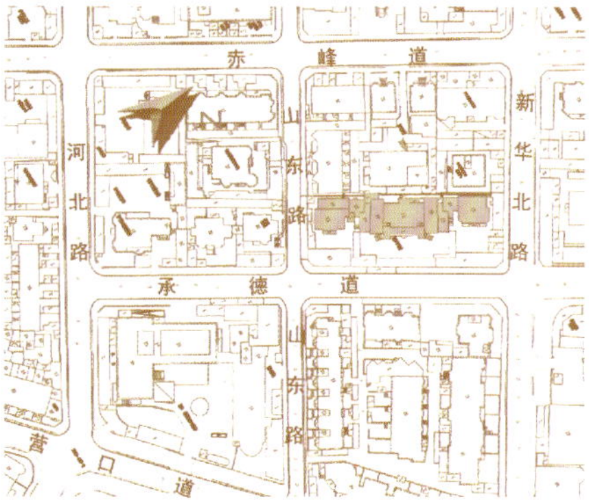

外景 Exterior view

外景 Exterior view

大门 Gate

屋顶栏杆 Balustrade on the roof

门廊 Portico

外景 Exterior view

老花池 Old-fashioned pond

外檐局部 Partial outer-eaves

外檐门 Gate under the outer-eaves

门厅 Lobby

走廊 Corridor

外景 Exterior view

# Former Chongde Hall
# 原崇德堂

原崇德堂位于和平区营口道24号、承德道17号，重点保护等级历史风貌建筑，现为居住、办公用房。崇德堂是法国天主教会负责在津经营教会产业及房地产的机构。该建筑建于1908年，占地面积约1 100m$^2$，建筑面积约2 000m$^2$，混合结构二层楼房，带半地下室。建筑平面为集合式住宅布局，附带小教堂。建筑立面以红砖为主，并用青砖砌筑拱券、壁柱及支撑拱券的圆柱，起到色彩强烈的装饰效果。半地下室由石材砌筑，首层由壁柱分隔形成二联拱券窗，二层为圆柱支撑的四联拱券窗，以此形成开敞的通廊，丰富了建筑造型。

正立面渲染图 Facade Rendering

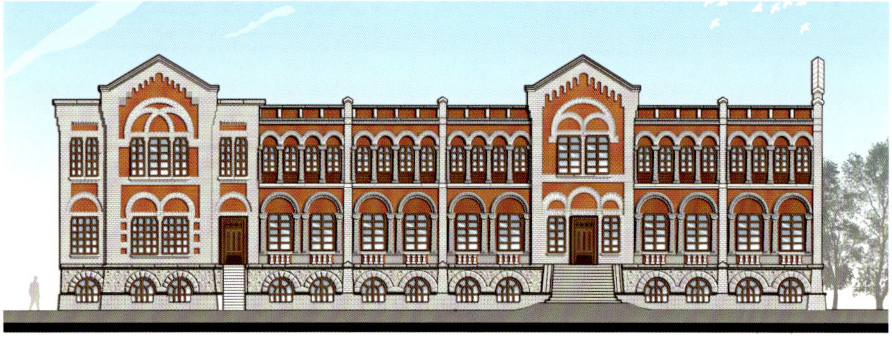

Located at 24 Yingkou Avenue,17 Chengde Avenue of Heping District, the Former Chongde Hall is an important protection historic architecture, and now residential and office building. Chongde Hall is an institution the French Catholic Church in Tianjin dealing in church industry and real estate business. Built in 1908, it covers an area of 1,100 square meters and a floor area of 2,000 square meters. It is a two-storied mixed structure with a semi-basement. The architectural plane is congregate housing with a small church. The elevation is mainly red bricks with black bricks laying arches, pilasters and columns propping the arches, creating a rich-colored decorative effect. The semi-basement is laid with stones. On the ground floor, pilasters separate and form two-arch windows. On the first floor, columns prop four-arch windows, and thus form an open corridor, which enriches the appearance of the building.

外檐细部 Details of the outer-eaves

入口 Entrance

外檐局部 Partial outer-eaves

原设计图 Original blueprint

外檐局部 Partial outer-eaves

外檐局部 Partial outer eaves

# Yi De Lane
# 义德里

义德里位于和平区陕西路与万全道交口，由六幢联排公寓形成里弄式住宅，一般保护等级历史风貌建筑，现为居住用房。该里弄建于1902年，占地面积约4 800 m$^2$，总建筑面积约8 500 m$^2$，由訾玉甫投资建设，并用其堂号“义德堂”命名。建筑为砖木结构二层楼房，部分三层。外檐立面为红砖清水墙，局部混水抹灰装饰。大筒瓦坡屋面，檐部出挑较大。每户为独立单元，前后均设小院，临街建筑入口为拱券式门洞。室内房间按照现代生活方式布局，功能齐全，装饰考究，木楼梯、木地板至今仍保持完好。该里弄具有中西合璧的折中主义建筑特征。

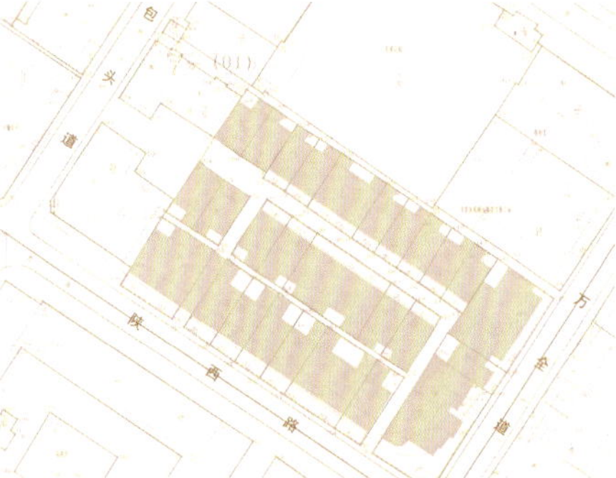

外景 Exterior view

单号正立面渲染图 Facade Rendering of the odd-numbered Building

单号左侧立面渲染图 Rendering of the left-side elevation of the odd-numbered Building

Located at the crossing of Shanxi Road and Wanquan Avenue of Heping District, Yi De Lane is a general protection historic architecture, constituted by six attached apartment buildings, and now residential. Built in 1902, it covers an area of 4,800 square meters and a floor area of 8,500 square meters. It was invested by Zi Yufu, and named after his company. The buildings are two-storied brick-timber structure, partially three-storied. They have fair-faced red-bricked external walls with partial plastered decorations, sloping roofs with large arched tiles and projected eaves. Each independent unit has its own front yard and back yard. The buildings that have street frontage have arched entrances. The rooms were designed according to modern life style with complete functions, elaborate decorations and well-preserved wooden staircases and floors. Yi De Lane, integrating Chinese and western architectural characteristics, has the features of eclectic architecture.

双号正立面渲染图 Facade Rendering of the even-numbered Building

里巷 Lane

外檐局部 Partial outer-eaves

里巷 Lane

双号主入口 Main entrance of the even-numbered Building

天花板 Ceiling

内檐门 Gate under the inner-eaves

外檐门 Door under the outer-eaves

# Henan Lane

# 河南里

河南里位于和平区河南路与营口道交口，由五幢联排公寓形成里弄式住宅，一般保护等级历史风貌建筑，现为居住用房。该里弄于1920年由湖北督军王占元投资建设，名仁和里，占地面积约4 600 $m^2$，总建筑面积约7 800 $m^2$。1982年，因其临近河南路而改为现名。该里弄建筑均为二层砖木结构楼房，每个单元独立，前后均设小院，首层设凸出平面的阳光房，二层为露台并有宝瓶栏杆装饰，入口均为拱券式。外檐大部分为混水墙面，局部清水。大筒瓦坡屋面，屋顶出老虎窗，起到通风采光的效果。室内房间按照现代生活方式布局，功能齐全，木楼梯、木地板、木门窗等装饰至今保存较好。

外景 Exterior view

里巷 Lane

Located at the crossing of Henan Road and Yingkou Avenue of Heping District, Henan Lane is a general protection historic architecture, constituted by five attached apartment buildings, and now residential. Built in 1920, it was invested by the governor of Hubei Province, Wang Zhanyuan and named Ren He Lane. It covers an area of 4,600 square meters and a floor area of 7,800 square meters. In 1982, its name changed to Henan Lane because of the road it was close to. The buildings are two-storied brick-timber structure. Each independent living unit has its own front yard and back yard. On the first floor there is a projected solarium while on the second floor there is a balcony with goblets railings as decorations. All the entrances are arched. The external walls are mostly plastered bricks walls with a small fair-faced part. The roofs are sloping with large arched tiles and projected dormant windows for ventilation and lighting. The rooms were designed according to modern life style with complete functions and well-preserved wooden staircases, floors, doors and windows.

里巷 Lane

# Anshan Avenue Area

# 鞍山道地区

修复后主楼外景 Exterior view of the renovated Main Building

# Jingyuan Garden
# 静园

静园位于和平区鞍山道70号，天津市文物保护单位，特殊保护等级历史风貌建筑，占地面积约3 000 $m^2$，建筑面积约1 900 $m^2$。静园原名乾园，为北洋政府驻日公使陆宗舆私邸，建于1921年。该建筑由主楼、图书馆、佣人房、厨房、车库组成。主楼为砖木结构二层楼房，局部三层。一楼为客厅、餐厅，二楼为卧室。室内为木楼梯、木地板。外檐为混水墙面，局部硫缸砖清水砖墙。建筑为多坡屋顶，红瓦屋面，各建筑之间由连廊相连，具有折中主义建筑特征。1929年末代皇帝溥仪迁居乾园，将“乾园”改名“静园”，取“静以养吾浩然之气”之意。1931年溥仪由此出逃到大连，后当上伪“满洲国”傀儡“皇帝”。

天津解放后，静园曾作为办公用房，后成为多户居民居住的大杂院。2005年10月，天津市国土资源和房屋管理局依据《天津市历史风貌建筑保护条例》对静园内45户居民进行了腾迁，拆除了院内的违章建筑，依照“修旧如故、安全适用”的原则，对静园进行复原整修。2007年7月，复原整修工程全部竣工，静园对社会开放。

主楼正立面渲染图 Facade rendering of the Main Building

修复前主楼 Main Building before renovation

主楼西立面彩图

Constructed in 1921, Jingyuan Garden is located at 70 Anshan Avenue, Heping District, listed as the heritage site under city protection and the important historic architecture under special protection in Tianjin. It covers an area of about 3,000 square meters, and its floor area was about 1,900 square meters. Originally named Qianyuan Garden, it was the private residence of Lu Zongyu, minister-counselor to Japan appointed by the Beiyang Warlords' Government. The complex consists of the main building, library, servants' chamber, kitchen and garage. The main brick-wood building is mainly two-storied while three-storied partially. The first floor serves for a living room and a dinning room, while the second floor for bedrooms. The stairways and floors are made of wood inside the building. The exterior walls are mainly stucco-finished but partially dried with glazed quarry tiles. With red-tiled sloping-roofs, all the buildings in the garden are linked by corridors. The whole complex looks typically eclectic.

Then in 1929, Qianyuan Garden was changed to Jingyuan Garden by Puyi, the last emperor of Qing Dynasty, when he settled here."Jing"means"stillness", and the Garden named after it in hint that the abdicated emperor would like to strengthen himself with noble spirit in a moveless environment. It was also from here that Puyi escaped to Dalian in 1931 and took the "crown" again.

After the liberation of Tianjin, Jingyuan Garden was used as the office building and then as a civil dwelling for many households. Well in October of 2005, the 45 households were

大门外景 Exterior view of Rear Gate

arranged to move out of the Garden and the unapproved structure not belonging to the original complex were demolished by the Land Resources and Housing Administration, Tianjin via the *Regulations on the Protection of Building of Historic Significance, Tianjin*. Restoration and renovation were initiated in line with the principle of "Restoring to its Original State and guaranteeing Safety and Applicability". And by July of 2007, the work had been completed and the Garden had reopened to the public.

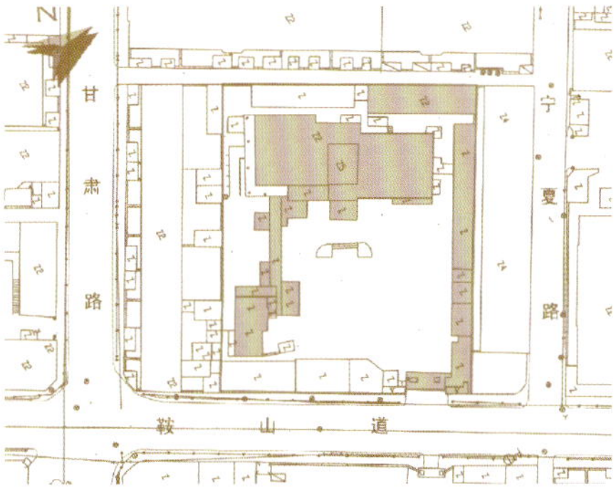

外景 Exterior view

夜景 Night view

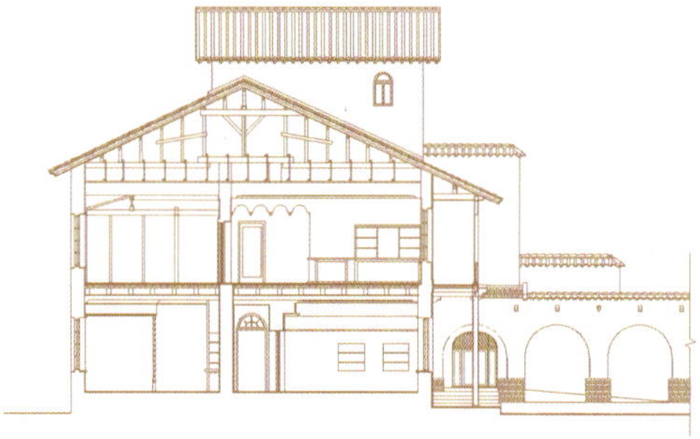

西跨院 Western Yard

门厅 Lobby

↓过厅 Passageway

客厅 Living Room

楼梯间 Staircase

三楼楼梯间 Stair Hall on third floor

书房 Study Room

卧室 Bedroom

餐厅 Dining Room

↓舞厅 Ballroom

# Former Residence of Mr.Zhang

# 张园

塔楼 Tower

张园位于和平区鞍山道59号，天津市文物保护单位，重点保护等级的历史风貌建筑，原是晚清武举张彪私邸，现为办公用房。张彪（1860—1927），字虎臣，山西榆次人，出身武举，赐总兵衔，曾任湖北营务处总办、标统、提督，后任驻武昌陆军第六镇统制。武昌起义爆发后，携眷逃往日本。1916年在天津原日租界建私宅“张园”寓居。1924年12月，孙中山先生赴京途中，曾下榻于此。末代皇帝溥仪被驱逐出宫后，于1925年来到天津，在此居住至1929年，而后迁居静园。“七七事变”后，张园被日本驻屯军占用并进行重建，作为驻屯军军官的官邸。

现存建筑为混合结构二层楼房（设有地下室），占地面积约6 700 $m^2$，建筑面积约3 300 $m^2$，建筑布局不对称，转角处设有塔楼，强调竖向构图。建筑借鉴意大利古典复兴造型，采用拱券窗、拱券入口门厅、高耸的塔楼等建筑元素，红瓦坡顶，清水砖墙，使得立面效果丰富、热烈。建筑内部装修考究，细部设计丰富。

↓外檐窗Windows below the outer-eaves

正立面渲染图 Facade Rendering

Located at 59 Anshan Avenue, Heping District, the Former Residence of Mr.Zhang is the heritage site under city protection and the important protection historic architecture. Formerly a private residence of Zhang Biao, a successful military candidate in the imperial provincial examination in late Qing Dynasty, it is presently an office building. Zhang Biao (1860–1927), with a courtesy name of Huchen, was born in Yuci, Shanxi Province. He was a successful military candidate in the imperial provincial examination and was granted a title of Garrison Commander. He was once the director of Hubei Troop Affairs Office, regimental commander, provincial commander-in-chief and then commander of the Sixth Army Division in Wuchang. After the outbreak of Wuchang Uprising, he carried his family members to flee to Japan. In 1916, he started to build his private residence "Zhangyuan Garden" in the Japanese concession in Tianjin to live. Mr. Sun Yat-sen had stayed here on his way to Peking in December 1924. The last emperor, Pu Yi, came to Tianjin in 1925 after being expelled from the Palace and lived in the place till moving to Jingyuan Garden in 1929. After the July 7th Incident, Zhangyuan Garden was occupied by Japanese garrison army and reconstructed as a mansion for garrison army officers.

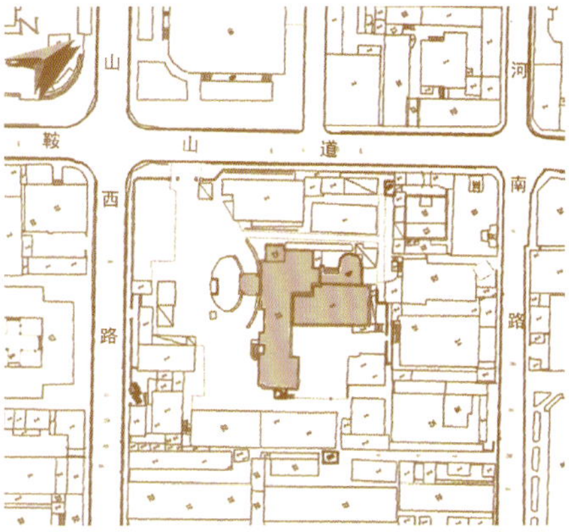


The existing construction is a two-storied building in mixed structure (with basements), covering an area of about 6,700 square meters and a floor area of about 3,300 square meters. The architectural composition is asymmetric with towers at corners and a focus on vertical composition. The building borrowed the Italian classical revival modeling and adopted architectural elements such as arch windows, arch entrance halls and steep towers. With red tiled sloping roofs and fair-faced walls, the building shows rich and strong facade effects. The interior decoration is carefully selected and the design of details is abundant.

主入口门廊 Main entrance Portico

外景 Exterior view

内景 Inner view

木雕细部
Detailed wood carving

楼梯 Stairs

一层走廊 Corridor on the first floor

彩色玻璃窗
Stained glass window

铁艺装饰 Iron artwork

老吊灯 Old-fashioned lamp

老壁灯 Old-fashioned wall lamp

壁炉 Fireplace

# Former Residence of Duan Qirui
# 段祺瑞旧宅

段祺瑞旧宅位于和平区鞍山道38号，天津市区、县文物保护单位，重点保护等级历史风貌建筑，现为办公用房。段祺瑞（1865—1936），字芝泉，安徽合肥人，皖系军阀首领。1885年段祺瑞考入天津武备学堂炮科，1889年毕业后赴德国军事院校学习炮兵科，并在克虏伯炮厂实习。1890年回国后，他先后在北洋军械局和随营武备学堂任职。1896年任小站新建陆军炮兵学堂总办兼炮兵第三营统带，与王士珍、冯国璋并称"北洋三杰"。辛亥革命后，他曾任民国政府陆军总长、国务总理，在1920年的直皖战争中被击败下台，寓居天津。1924年第二次直奉战争后，直系军阀失败，段祺瑞重掌大权，就任"中华民国临时执政"；1926年被冯玉祥驱逐，再次寓居天津，1933年移居上海。

该建筑建于1920年，占地面积约3 200 $m^2$，建筑面积约3 100 $m^2$，为混合结构的三层楼房（设有地下室）。建筑布局以西方生活方式为参考，首层为起居、会客、舞厅、餐厅等公共空间，二、三层为卧室等私密空间。建筑造型为对称的古典复兴式，混水墙面，一、二层均设有开敞柱廊，采用简易古罗马柱式，入口处设有条石高台阶，建筑庄严气派。

外景 Exterior view

Located at 38 Anshan Avenue, Heping District, the Former Residence of Duan Qirui is the heritage site under city/county protection and the important protection historic architecture and is currently used as an office building. Duan Qirui (1865–1936) with a courtesy name of Zhiquan and born in Hefei, Anhui Province, was the leader of the Wan Xi warlords. In 1885, he passed the examination and entered into the Artillery Department of Tianjin Military School. After his graduation in 1889, he was sent to a Germany military college to study artillery and practiced in Krupp Works. After returning to China in 1890, he took office in the Beiyang Armory and the Military Staff Academy successively. In 1896, he was named as the director of the Artillery Academy of the New Army in Xiaozhan and the artillery commander. He was known as one of the "Three Outstanding Persons of Beiyang", including Wang Shizhen and Feng Guozhang. After the Revolution of 1911, he was named as minister of war and then premier in the government of the Republic of China. He was defeated and forced to step down during the Zhili-Anhui War in 1920, then he moved to Tianjin and lived there. When the Zhi Xi failed in the second Zhili-Fengtian War in 1924, Duan Qirui regained the power and took the post of "Temporary Chief Executive of the Republic of China". He was exiled by Feng Yuxiang in 1926 and lived in Tianjin again, moving to Shanghai in 1933.

Built in 1920, the three-storied building (with basements) in mixed structure covers an area of about 3,200 square meters and a floor area of about 3,100 square meters. The architectural composition is in a western living style: the first floor consists of common spaces for sitting, reception, dancing and dinning etc; the second and third floors are private spaces such as bedrooms. The architectural modeling is a symmetrical classic revival: furred walls, open porticos supported by simple ancient Roman columns in the first and second floors, high steps paved by block stones at the entrance, all presenting solemnity and magnificence.

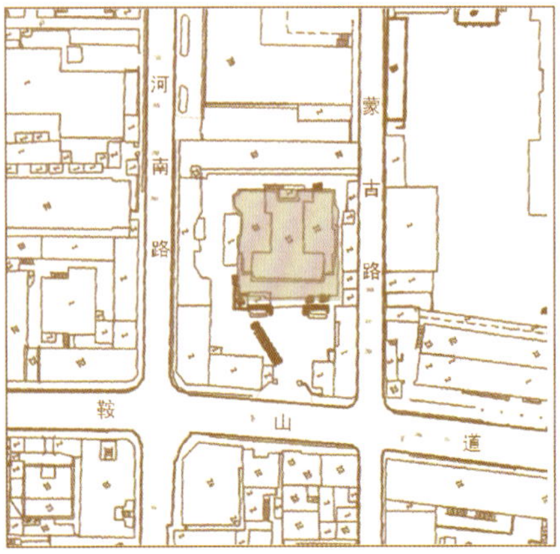

主入口 Main entrance

主入口内景 Inner view of the main entrance

内景 Inner view

内景 Inner view

内景 Inner view

内景 Inner view

二层天花板 Ceiling of second floor

内檐门 Gate under the inner eaves

一层护墙板 Wall-panels on the first floor

楼梯 Stairs

二层内景 Inner view of the second floor

二楼阳台廊柱 Columns on the balcony of second floor

二楼阳台廊柱 Columns on the balcony of second floor

# Xin Jia Lane

# 新佳里

新佳里位于和平区蒙古路与多伦道交口，由平面对称的两幢联排式住宅组成，一般保护等级历史风貌建筑，现为居住用房。该建筑位于原日租界，建于1926年，为日租界警察署宿舍，占地面积约900 m²，总建筑面积约1 200 m²。1946年更名“新兴里”，1982年改为现名称。建筑为砖木结构二层楼房，两幢建筑平行设置，中间留通道，楼后设有小院。每幢建筑平面两端半圆形突出部分为楼梯间。外檐立面为“甩疙瘩”抹灰饰面，主入口上方均设雨篷。建筑整体朴实无华，无过多装饰。

正立面渲染图 Facade Rendering

外檐局部 Partial outer-eaves

外檐局部 Partial outer-eaves

Located at the crossing of Monggu Road and Duolun Avenue of Heping District, Xin Jia Lane is a general protection historic architecture, constituted by two symmetrical attached apartment buildings, and now residential. Built in 1926, it was in Japanese concession and was the dormitory of the policemen of the concession. It covers an area of 900 square meters and a total floor area of 1,200 square meters. In 1946, its name changed to Xin Xing Lane, and in 1982, to the present name. It is a two-storied brick-timber structure. The two buildings are paralleling with a gallery in between and a yard in the back. The semicircle projections on both sides of each building are staircases. The external walls are plastered with decorative lumps. Canopies are set above main entrances. The architecture is plain and simple without excessive decorations.

外景 Exterior view

# One-Palace Garden Area

# 一宫花园地区

# Former Residence of the Yuan's Family
# 袁氏旧宅

袁氏旧宅位于河北区海河东路39号，天津市文物保护单位，特殊保护等级历史风貌建筑，现为商业用房。这是袁世凯族侄袁乃宽为袁世凯督建的住宅，但住宅未完工，袁世凯已暴死。袁乃宽（1868—？），河南项城人，出身县学生，历任天津知县、镶红旗蒙古副都统等职。曾参与袁世凯复辟帝制活动，一度出任农商总长，去职后寓居天津。

该建筑建于1918年，占地面积约1 800m²，建筑面积约2 100m²，主楼为混合结构三层楼房（附楼二层），红瓦坡顶，混水墙面。建筑造型独特，装饰繁多，有荷兰滨水建筑特征；中部的六角形塔楼成为构图中心；建筑室内设隐身处和逃生处，逃生暗道上达屋顶露台，下通海河，布局独特；面向海河设八角形观景房和风水窗，可观四时风景，寓意吉祥。

外檐局部 Partial outer-eaves

The Former Residence of Yuan Shikai, which is now a commercial building, is located at 39 East Haihe Road, Hebei District, classified as the heritage site under city protection and the special protection historic architecture in Tianjin. The resident was built under the supervision of Yuan Naikuan(1868–?), nephew of Yuan Shikai. It was originally for Yuan Shikai, but he died before its completion. Born in Xiangcheng County of Henan Province, Yuan Naikuan had been the supporter for his uncle to restore the monarchy and served once the Minister of Agriculture and Commerce. He served as Magistrate of Tianjin and Vice Governor of Bordered Red Banner, Mongolia, successively. He moved to settle in Tianjin after his retirement.

The resident was built in 1918. It covers an area of about 1,800 square meters, and its floor area was about 2,100 square meters. With its red-tiled sloping roofs and stucco finished walls, the main building of the residence is

正立面渲染图 Facade Rendering

左侧立面渲染图 Rendering of the left-side elevation

夜景 Night view

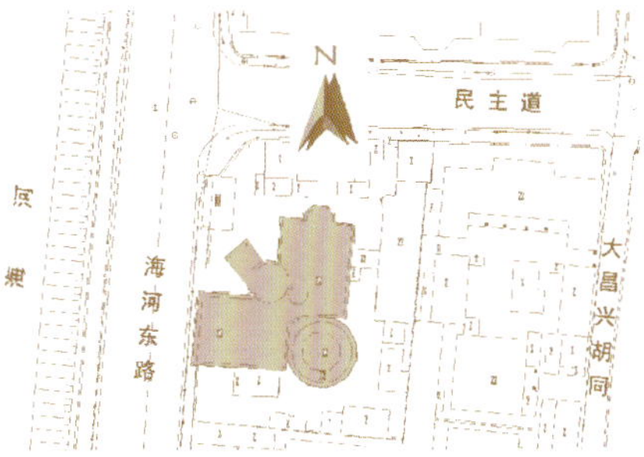


a composite three-storied structure while the Annex being two-storied. It is characterized as the architecture of the waterfront considering its unique style and rich decorations. A hexagon towered section serves as the central point of the building. Moreover the secret room and safety passage were designed in the building. Especially the safety passage was leading its way up to the terrace on the roof and down to the Haihe River at a distance. Facing the River, the octagon room was designed purposely with landscape windows for people to enjoy the views along with lucks al! the year round.

外景 Exterior view

首府酒

内景 Inner view

内景 Inner view

内景 Inner view

内景 Inner view

内檐局部 Partial under the inner-eaves

内檐局部 Partial under the inner-eaves

室内柱 Columns under the inner-eaves

室内柱 Columns under the inner-eaves

楼梯 Stairs

# Former Residence of Feng Guozhang

# 冯国璋旧宅

冯国璋旧宅位于河北区民主道50～54号，天津市区、县文物保护单位，特殊保护等级历史风貌建筑，现为办公用房。冯国璋（1857—1919），字华甫，河北河间人，直系军阀首领，毕业于天津武备学堂。辛亥革命后出任直隶都督、江苏都督。1916年他当选为副总统；1917年任代理大总统；1918年去职，寓居天津、北京，曾在天津投资金融、工业、矿业及房地产。

该建筑建于1912年，占地面积约700 $m^2$，建筑面积约1 900 $m^2$，由奥地利建筑师布吕纳设计建造。建筑为砖木结构二层楼房，呈对称布局，中央盔顶部分为视觉中心，两端三角山花又加强了这种构图形式。建筑体量适宜、舒展，色彩搭配协调统一。

Located at 50～54 Minzhu Avenue of Hebei District, the Former Residence of Feng Guozhang is the heritage site under city/county protection and the special protection historic architecture, and now an office building. Feng Guozhang 1857–1919 with a coutesy name Huafu, born in Hejian of Hebei Province, was a head of Zhi Xi warlord. He graduated from Tianjin Military School, and served as the governor of Zhili and the governor of Jiangsu Province after the Revolution of 1911. In 1916, he was elected the vice president of the Republic of China. In 1917, he was the acting president. In 1918, he left the post and lived in Tianjin and Beijing. He used to invest in finance, industry, mining and real estate. Built in 1912, his former residence covers an area of 700 square meters and a floor area of 1,900 square meters. Designed by an Austrian architect, it is a two-storied brick-timber structure. The layout is bilaterally symmetrical with the central top as the visual center. The triangle pediments on both sides enforce the symmetry. The building has a proper size which harmonizes well with the color collocation.

外景 Exterior view

外檐局部 Partial outer-eaves

主入口 Main entrance

盔顶 Helmet-shaped roof

右侧立面渲染图Rendering of the right-side elevation

正立面渲染图 Facade Rendering

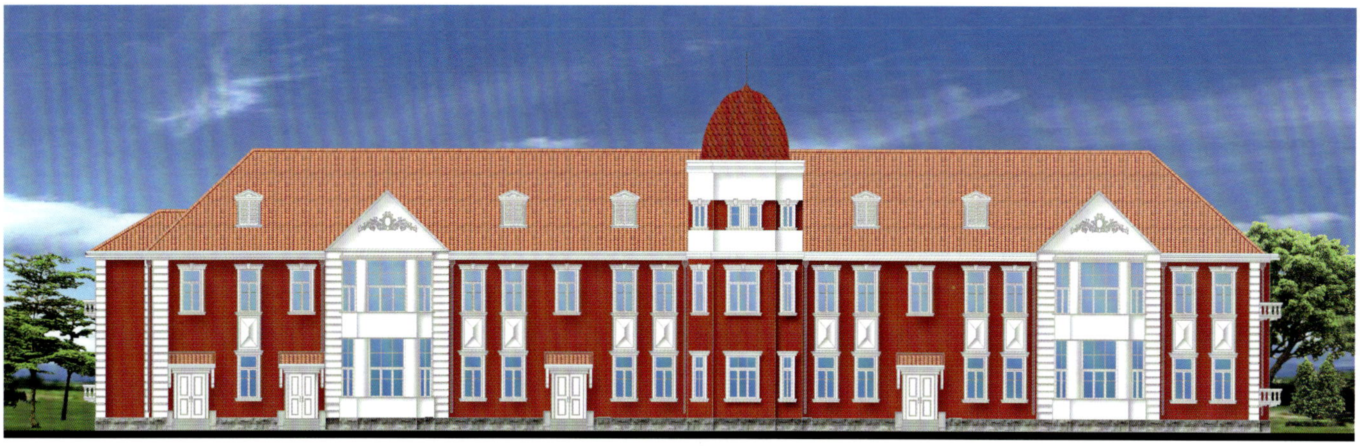

# Former Residence of Liang Qichao

# 梁启超旧宅

梁启超旧宅、“饮冰室”书斋位于河北区民族路44~46号，占地面积约2 500 $m^2$，全国重点文物保护单位，重点保护等级历史风貌建筑，现为纪念馆。梁启超（1873—1929），广东新会人，中国近代著名思想家和学者，清末与康有为共同发动“公车上书”，主张维新。辛亥革命后他先后出任司法总长、财政部长等职，1915年定居天津。他反对袁世凯称帝，并与云南督军蔡锷在天津共同策划反袁武装起义，在五四运动中倡导“诗界革命”、“小说革命”和白话文。

其旧宅位于河北区民族路44号，建于1914年，建筑面积约1 000 $m^2$。砖木结构二层楼房（设有地下室），设有开敞柱廊，东侧转角处的八角形角楼成为最主要的竖向构图。“饮冰室”书斋位于民族路46号，建于1924年，建筑面积约900 $m^2$，意大利建筑师白罗尼欧设计，砖木结构二层楼房（设有地下室）。建筑平面布局为“凹”字形，强调对称构图，装饰较多且造型复杂。建筑体量厚重敦实，带有古典主义色彩。

饮冰室外景 Exterior view of Yinbingshi

外景 Exterior view

Being the important heritage site under state protection and the important protection historic architecture in Tianjin, the former Residence of Liang Qichao and his Studio, Yinbingshi, are located respectively at 44~46 Minzu Road, Heibei District, and cover an area of about 2,500 square meters. The site is a museum nowadays. Born in Xinhui County of Guangdong Province, Liang Qichao (1873–1929) is regarded as one of the most famous ideologists and scholars in modern China. It was he who submitted the Joint Petition of Imperial Examination Candidates to the Emperor along with Kang Youwei, calling for the social reform in China. After the Revolution of 1911, he was appointed as the ministers of Judiciary and Finance one after the other. He moved to settle in Tianjin in 1915. He fought against the restoration of monarchy by Yuan Shikai and further planned to launch an anti-Yuan uprising with General Cai E, Military Governor of Yunnan Province. He also made his efforts to bring the reformations to the areas of poetry, novel and language.

The former Residence of Liang was built in 1924, at 44 Minzu Road, and its floor area was about 1,000 square meters. The brick-wood building is two-storied along with its basement and open colonnade. The octagonal pavilion at the east corner serves as the major vertical structure of the architecture. Designed by Bironio, an Italian architect, and sitting at 46 Minzu Road, his Studio, Yinbingshi, was constructed in 1924, and its floor area was about 900 square meters. This brick-wood structure was composed in a symmetrically concave plan, rich in shapes and decorations and with the basement as well. It looks massive and steady, presenting with Classicism.

雪景 Snow viewv

梁启超纪念馆

饮冰室客厅 Living Room of Yinbingshi

楼梯 Stairs

饮冰室采光穹顶 Lighting Dome of Yinbingshi

饮冰室内景 Inner view of Yinbingshi

饮冰室书房内景 Inside the Study Room of Yinbingshi

饮冰室顶棚 Ceiling of Yinbingshi

饮冰室客厅 Living Room of Yinbingshi

↓饮冰室卧室 Bedroom of Yinbingshi

# Former Residence of Zhang Mingqi

# 张鸣岐旧宅

张鸣岐旧宅位于河北区民族路80号，重点保护等级历史风貌建筑，现为办公用房。张鸣岐（1875—1945），字坚白，山东无棣人，1894年甲午科举人，曾任广西巡抚、两广总督兼广州将军。1911年他率兵镇压了黄兴领导的黄花岗起义，杀害了林觉民等革命志士。袁世凯称帝失败后，张鸣岐寓居天津，购此建筑并居住，1928年后迁居英租界。

该建筑为原意租界马可波罗广场周边三组花园别墅中的一幢，占地面积约700 m²，建筑面积约500 m²，为砖木结构带地下室的二层楼房。二层屋顶设休闲露台，局部三层设塔亭，体现了主人崇洋闲适的生活。外檐为混水墙面，平顶出大挑檐，挑檐下的悬挑支撑、窗套、露台栏杆、塔亭的圆柱三联拱等细部构件，造型精致独特。建筑整体外观精巧典雅。

马可波罗广场 Marco Polo Square

雪景 Snow view

Located at Minzu Road, Hebei District, the Former Residence of Zhang Mingqi is an important protection historic architecture and is now an office building. Born in Wudi, Shangdong Province, Zhang Mingqi (1875–1945) had a courtesy name of Jianbai, a successful candidate in the imperial examinations at the provincial level in 1894. He had been appointed governor of Guangxi Province, viceroy of Guangxi and Guangdong and meanwhile Guangzhou General. He suppressed Huanghuagang Uprising led by Huang Xing in 1911 and killed revolutionary persons including Lin Juemin. When Yuan Shikai failed after proclaiming himself emperor, Zhang Mingqi lived in Tianjin, purchased this building and resided here. He moved to the British concession in 1928.

The building was originally one of the three garden villas around Marco Polo Square in the Italian concession, covering an area of about 700 square meters and a floor area of about 500 square meters and being a two-storied brick-timber building with a basement. There is a terrace for leisure on the roof of the second floor; part of the third floor has a tower, indicating the host's worship of the western leisure life. The exterior wall is plastered bricked and the flat roof has large cornices. The detailed components including the overhanging braces, window pocket, terrace handrails and the three continuous arches with columns are all delicate and unique in modeling. The overall appearance of the building is delicate and elegant.

正立面渲染图 Facade Rendering

左侧立面渲染图Rendering of the left-side elevation

外景 Exterior view

# Former Residence of Bao Guiqing

# 鲍贵卿旧宅

鲍贵卿旧宅位于河北区平安街81号，重点保护等级历史风貌建筑，现为办公用房。鲍贵卿（1866—1934），字霆九，辽宁海城人，天津北洋武备学堂工程科毕业，曾任北洋政府陆军总长、黑龙江督军、吉林督军等职，下野后寓居天津。他于1920—1921年购得此楼并改建成一座豪华的花园住宅。

该建筑为混合结构二层楼房，局部三层，带地下室，多坡瓦屋顶。外檐为青砖清水墙面。一、二层设柱廊，三层局部退台形成大露台，露台上建有三个风格迥异的亭子，中间为带有罗曼式屋顶和简化科林斯柱式的西洋凉亭，东面为中国传统的圆攒尖亭，西面为较简洁的西洋凉亭。室内装饰豪华。中西合璧的建筑设计，印证了当时天津中西文化交融的情况。

Located at 81 Ping'an Street of Hebei District, the Former Residence of Bao Guiqing is an important protection historic architecture and now an office building. Bao Guiqing 1866–1934 with a coutesy name Tingjiu, born in Haicheng, Liaoning Province and graduated from Tianjin Beiyang Military School, majoring in engineering. He used to be the Chief of Army in the Beiyang Warlord Government, warlord of Heilongjiang Province and Jilin Province. He lived in Tianjin after falling out of power. He purchased the building from 1920 to 1921 and renovated it into a luxurious garden house.

It is a two-storied and partially three-storied mixed structure with a basement and multi-tile sloping roofs. The external is fair-faced black-bricked wall. Colonnades are set on the first floor and the second floor. On the third floor there is a big balcony with three pavilions on it which are different in style. In the middle is a western pavilion with a Roman roof and simplified Corinthian columns. On the east is a traditional Chinese pavilion with a conical roof while on the west is a simple western pavilion. Inside the house are luxurious decorations. The architectural design is an evidence of the combination of Chinese and western cultures in Tianjin then.

外景 Exterior view

外景 Exterior view

认真贯彻落实科学

屋顶凉亭 Summerhouse on the roof

内檐门 Gate under the inner-eaves

主入口 Main entrance

二楼阳台门 Door on the balcony of the second floor

精美的木雕 Exquisite wood-carvings

楼梯 Stairs

# Former Residence of Tang Yulin

# 汤玉麟旧宅

汤玉麟旧宅位于河北区民主道40号，天津市文物保护单位，重点保护等级历史风貌建筑，占地面积约2 600m$^2$，建筑面积约3 200m$^2$为北洋政府交通总长吴毓麟于1922年建造的私宅，后卖与汤玉麟。汤玉麟（1871~1949），山东人，出身绿林，曾任热河省政府主席兼第三十六师师长，去职后寓居天津。该建筑为混合结构二层楼房，红瓦坡顶，平面布局严谨对称，立面装饰丰富，做工精美，开窗形式多样，具有折中主义建筑特征。

As the heritage site under city protection and the important protection historic architecture in Tianjin, the Former Residence of Tang Yulin sits at 40 Minzhu Avenue, Hebei District. It covers an area of about 2,600 square meters, and a floor area of about 3,200 square meters. It was originally built in 1922 by Wu Yulin, Minister of Communications for the Beiyang Warlords' Government and then purchased by Tang Yulin in 1930 as his resident.

Tang Yulin (1871-1949) came from

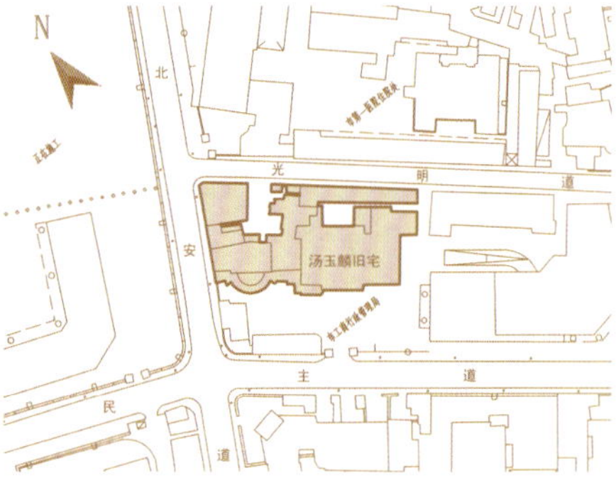

外檐局部 Partial outer-eaves

外檐局部 Partial outer-eaves

Shandong Province, once being a bandit and then the commander of the 36th Division and even the governor of Rehe Province. He settled in Tianjin after his retirement.

This composite structure is two-storied with red-tiled sloping roofs. It was laid out in a strictly symmetrical style. Rich in ornaments under the outer-eaves and windows in different shapes, the architecture taste delicate and presents with an eclectic atmosphere.

外檐细部 Details of the outer-eaves

外檐窗 Window under the outer-eaves

外景 Exterior view

内景 Inner view

# Former Residence of Liu Rangong

# 刘髯公旧宅

刘髯公旧宅位于河北区建国道66号，重点保护等级历史风貌建筑，现为办公用房。刘髯公（1893—1938），字仲儒，天津武清人，回族，曾任法国驻华使馆文书，天津法租界工部局侦探长。1924年他与段松坡、薛月楼合作，创办《新天津报》，以“平民化”、“敢说话”为标榜，以整版篇幅连载《三侠剑》等长篇评书小说，报纸行销远及东北、西北各地。此后他们还陆续发行了《新天津晚报》、《新天津小报》等六种报刊。天津沦陷前，《新天津报》宣传抗日，甚为激烈。1937年8月刘髯公被日寇逮捕，严刑拷打，后经天津各清真寺大寺阿訇联名具结保外就医，不久逝世。

该建筑占地面积约2 300m$^2$，建筑面积约3 600m$^2$，砖木结构二层楼房，带半地下室，清水墙面，坡屋顶，瓦屋面，上设老虎窗，一、二层均设圆柱外廊。建筑尺度适宜，豪华大气，具有折中主义建筑特征。

外景 Exterior view

外檐局部 Partial outer-eaves

外檐局部 Partial outer eaves

Located at 66 Jianguo Avenue, Hebei District, the Former Residence of Liu Rangong is an important protection historic architecture and is now an office building. Liu Rangong (1893–1938), with a courtesy name of Zhongru, was born in Wuqing, Tianjin, in a Muslim family. He was once clerical assistant in the Embassy of France in China and Chief Inspector of Municipal Council in the French concession in Tianjin. Cooperating with Duan Songpo and Xue Yuelou, he founded *New Tientsin* in 1924, famous for being "civilian oriented" and "bold to say". The newspaper made use of a full page to serialize long stories and novels such as *San Xia Jian*. It was well sold, even to the northeast and northwest regions. Thereafter, they issued six newspapers/magazines including *New Tientsin Evening Paper and New Tientsin Tabloid* etc. Before Tianjin was occupied by the Japanese troops, *New Tientsin* propagandized fighting against the Japanese strongly. Liu Rangong was arrested by the Japanese troops in August 1937 and tortured cruelly, later released on bail for medical service upon the recognizance made by Imams of major mosques in Tianjin.

The two-storied brick-timber building with basements covers an area of about 2,300 square meters and a floor area of about 3,600 square meters, with fair-faced walls, sloping tiled roofs with dormers and columned veranda in the frist and second floor. The architectural scale is appropriate, showing luxury and grandness with an architectural feature of eclecticism.

外檐窗 Windows below the outer-eaves

外檐门 Gate under the outer-eaves

外檐窗 Windows below the outer-eaves

走廊 Corridor

外檐局部 Partial outer-eaves

# South Jeifang Road Area
# 解放南路地区

# Former Residence of Wu Yulin

# 吴毓麟旧宅

吴毓麟旧宅位于河西区解放南路292号，天津市文物保护单位，重点保护等级历史风貌建筑，现为办公用房。吴毓麟（1871—1944），字秋舫，天津人，北洋水师学堂毕业，曾任大沽造船所所长、津浦铁路局局长。1923年他出任北洋政府交通总长，1924年退居津门，投资实业。吴毓麟最初居住在意租界现民主道40号（后将该宅卖与汤玉麟），后又租住了这幢著名实业家庄乐峰1931年建造的住宅。

该建筑占地面积约3 300 m²，建筑面积约2 700 m²，砖木结构三层楼房（三层为屋顶间坡顶），带地下室，多坡瓦屋顶，角部有四锥形小塔楼，外轮廓线丰富。外檐为混水墙面，于入口、窗间、檐口等处设精美浮雕装饰。阳台用每组五个连续圆孔造型形成护栏，风格独特。室内装饰豪华，门厅内设大理石喷泉，做工精美，窗户镶嵌彩色玻璃，厅内拱顶上有人兽混合图案的彩绘。

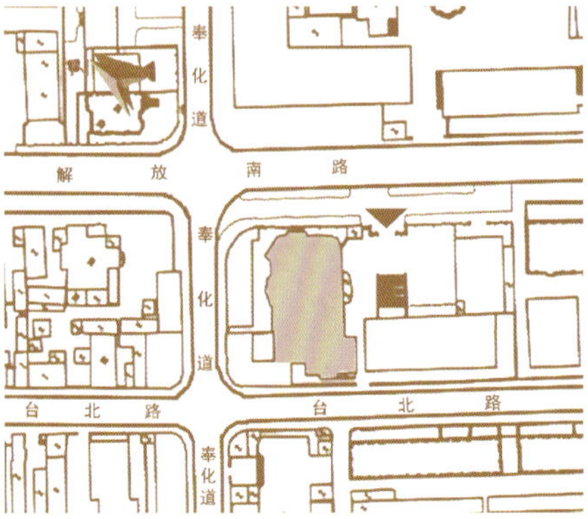

外景 Exterior view

Located at 292 South Jiefang Road, Hexi District, the Former Residence of Wu Yulin is the heritage site under city protection and the important protection historic architecture and now serves as an office. Wu Yulin (1871–1944), courtesy-named Qiufang, was born in Tianjin. Graduating from Beiyang Naval School, he was named director of Dagu Shipyard and director of Jin-Pu Railway Bureau. In 1923, he was appointed Minister of Transportation in Beiyang government and left for Tianjin in 1924 to invest in industry. At first, Wu Yulin resided in the Italian concession, currently 40 Minzhu Avenue (later he sold the house to Tang Yulin) and then rented the house built by famous industrialist Zhuang Lefeng in 1931.

The three-storied (the third floor being roof and pitched roofs) brick-timber building with basements covers an area of about 3,300 square meters and a floor area of about 2,700 square meters. The tiled roofs with many slopes and four-sided tapering towers at corners form rich outlines. The exterior walls are plastered brick walls, containing exquisite anaglyphs at entrance, among windows and on cornice. Five continuous round holes in each group form the guardrails of the balconies, unique in style. The interior decoration is luxurious, with a marble fountain with fine workmanship located at the hallway, windows installed with stained glass and vault in the hall drawn with men and animals.

外檐柱头 Column capital under the outer-eaves

↓柱础 Column base

外檐局部 Partial outer-eaves

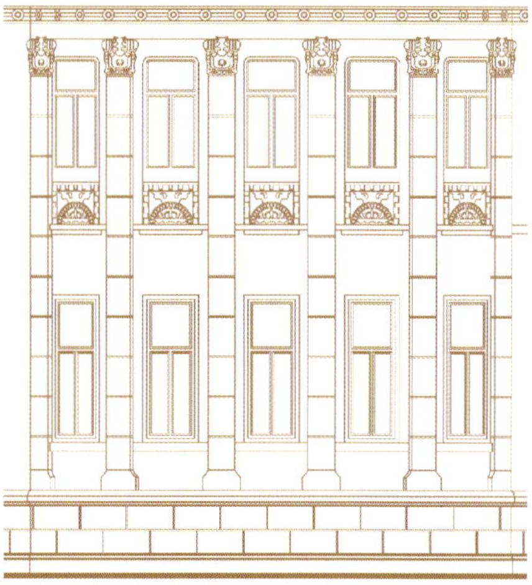

主入口地面 Floor at the Main entrance

楼梯 Stairs

楼梯 Stairs

大厅内景 Inner view of the Lobby

彩色玻璃窗 Stained glass window

大理石座椅 Marble bench

精美的石雕 Exquisite stone-carvings

屋顶 Ceiling

# Former German Courtyard

# 原德国大院

原德国大院位于河西区福建路与温州道交口，为相同风格的五幢联排公寓形成的建筑组团，一般保护等级历史风貌建筑，现为居住用房。该建筑组团位于原德租界，占地面积约3 900 m$^2$，总建筑面积约4 900 m$^2$，建于1923年，为德国侨民公寓，故称“德国大院”。建筑单体均为二层砖木结构楼房，带地下室，前后有院，室内木楼梯、木地板、木门窗，玻璃窗外加设百叶窗。外檐一层为清水墙，上部为“甩疙瘩”砂浆饰面。大筒瓦坡屋面，前后挑檐，挑檐望板做成似中国钱币的圆形方孔造型，利于通风防潮。入口上部均设有瓦顶雨厦。该建筑组团平面呈周边式布置，中间为花坛绿地，建筑整齐排列于四周，组团内部较为封闭，仅有一条甬道与外部相通，形成较安静舒适的居住环境。

历史照片 Historic photo

Located at the crossing of Fujian Road and Wenzhou Avenue of Hexi District, the Former German Courtyard is a general protection historic architecture, constituted by five attached apartment buildings of same style, and now residential. It was in German concession. It covers an area of 3,900 square meters and a floor area of 4,900 square meters. Built in 1923, it used to be the apartment buildings for German emigrants. That's how it got the name. All buildings are two-storied brick-timber structure with basements, front yards and back yards. Indoors there are wooden staircases, floors, doors and windows, glass windows with blinds. On the first floor, the external walls are fair-faced with mortar lumps as decorative finish. The buildings have sloping roofs with large arched tiles and projecting eaves in the front and at the back. The roof boarding is in the shape of ancient Chinese coins, round with a square hole in the center, for ventilation and moisture proofing. There are tiled canopies above each entrance. The group of buildings is peripheral-type, closing the flower bed in. Inside, there is only one passage connecting to the outside, forming a living environment quite quiet and comfortable.

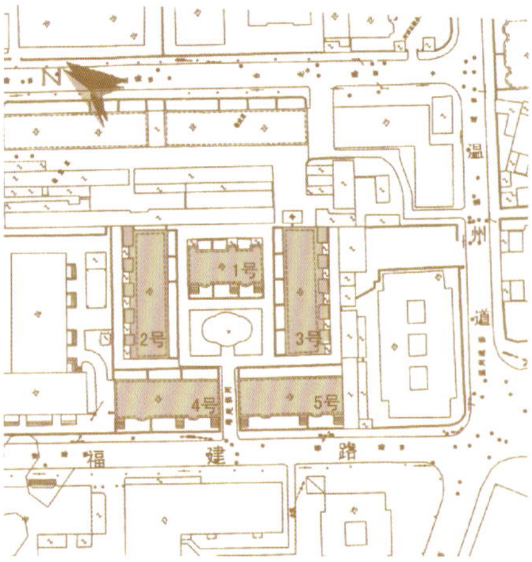


1号楼正立面渲染图 Facade Rendering of No.1 Building

2号楼正立面渲染图 Facade Rendering of No.2 Building

里巷 Lane

↓外景 Exterior view

1号楼外景 Exterior view of No.1 Building

外檐局部 Partial outer-eaves

入口 Entrance

外檐局部 Partial outer-eaves

外檐局部 Partial outer-eaves

# Former Residence of Wang Zhilong

# 王郅隆旧宅

王郅隆旧宅位于河西区浦口道22号，天津市文物保护单位，重点保护等级历史风貌建筑，现为办公用房。王郅隆（1888—1923），天津人。他出身商人，善经营，因与安徽督军倪嗣冲结识，并受皖系军阀徐树铮重用，先后任黑龙江、湖北、安徽等省盐务采运局总办，安武军后路局总办；后投资井陉等煤矿，创办天津华昌、丹华火柴公司，组织长顺盐业公司，与人合办金城银行、裕元纱厂、边业银行、《大公报》等。1918年王郅隆任安福系国会议员及北洋政府财政总长，被视为安福系军阀的“财神”。1920年皖系失败，王郅隆受到直系军阀通缉，辗转逃往日本，1923年死于日本关东大地震。

该建筑建于1900年，占地面积约5 200m²，建筑面积约2 500m²，砖木结构二层、局部三层楼房，设有地下室。红瓦坡顶，浅色混水墙面，主入口处用两组双柱支撑折角门廊，气势雄伟，体形错落有致。整幢建筑体现了德国民居和西洋古典建筑的混合风格。

外景 Exterior view

历史照片 Historic photo

Located at 22 Pukou Avenue, Hexi District, the Former Residence of Wang Zhilong is the heritage site under city protection and the important protection historic architecture and is now an office building. Wang Zhilong (1888–1923), born in Tianjin, was a businessmen and good at managing. Due to his acquaintance with Ni Sichong, the provincial military governor of Anhui Province, and the trust by Xu Shuzheng, a warlord of Wan Xi, he was appointed directors of Salt Purchase and Transportation Bureaus in Heilongjiang, Hubei and Anhui successively, and also director of Logistics Bureau in Anwu Army. Later, he invested in coal mines such as Jingjing, founded Tianjin Huachang and Danhua Match Company, organized Changshun Salt Company and jointly ventured Kinchen Bank, Yuyuan Cotton Mill, Bianye Bank and *Dagong Newspaper* etc. In 1918 he was named congressman of Anfu Xi and Financial Minister of Beiyang Government, being regarded as the "God of Wealth" for Anfu Xi. In 1920, the Wan Xi was defeated and Wang Zhilong was wanted for arrest by the Zhi Xi. He fled to Japan and died in Great Kanto Earthquake in 1923.

The two-storied (partially three-storied, with basements) brick-timber building was built in 1900, with covering an

area of about 5,200 square meters and a floor area of about 2,500 square meters. Red-tiled sloping roofs, light-colored plastered brick walls and a bevel porch supported by two groups of double columns at the main entrance display a majestic vigor and a well-arranged form. The whole building presents a mixed style of German folk house and western classical architecture.

正立面渲染图 Facade rendering

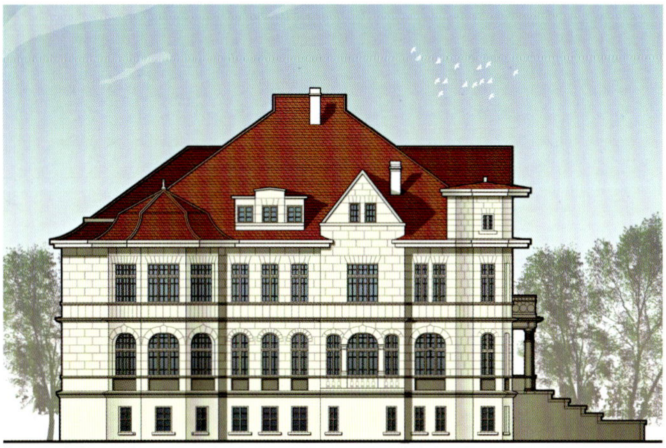

左侧立面渲染图Rendering of the left-side elevation

外景 Exterior view

院内凉亭 Summerhouse in the courtyard

↓凉亭藻井 Coffered ceiling of the Summerhouse

一楼门厅 Lobby on the first floor

内檐窗细部 Details of the window under the inner-eaves

楼梯间 Staircase

内景 Inner view

木雕护墙板 Wooden wall-panels

一楼会议室内护墙板 Wall-panels in the meeting room on the first floor

外景 Exterior view

# Former Residence of Zhang Xun

# 张勋旧宅

张勋旧宅位于河西区浦口道6号，天津市文物保护单位，重点保护等级历史风貌建筑，现为办公用房。张勋（1854—1923），江西人，出身行伍，积功至参将；1895年参加小站练兵，任工兵营管带，后升至总兵。1902年他奉调至北京，守卫紫禁城端门，嗣后擢为云南提督、甘肃提督、江南提督、江苏巡抚兼署理两江总督、南洋大臣。辛亥革命后，张勋表示仍效忠清室，所部一律保留辫发，他遂有“辫帅”之称，曾任江苏督军、长江巡阅使。1917年张勋利用大总统黎元洪与国务卿段祺瑞的“府院之争”，以“调解”为名，率军进入北京，拥戴溥仪复辟，自封为议政大臣、直隶总督兼北洋大臣。复辟失败后，他寓居天津，曾被任为热河林垦督办，但未就职。在天津他曾投资金融业，并建有大片房产。

旧宅为两幢独立二层砖木结构楼房，建于二十世纪初，占地面积约15 100 $m^2$，建筑面积约5 100 $m^2$，由德国工程师考特、鲁斯·凯甘尔设计。红瓦坡顶，混水墙面，室内装修考究。两楼以开敞柱廊相连接，建筑体量轻盈，色彩搭配协调。

2号楼外景 Exterior view of No.2 Building

The Former Residence of Zhang Xun is located at 6 Pukou Avenue, Hexi District. It has been classified as the heritage site under city protection and the important protection historic architecture in Tianjin. It covers an area of about 15,100 square meters and its floor area is about 5,100 square meters, and it is used as an office building now. Zhang Xun (1854–1923), born in Jiangxi Province, rose from the ranks and was promoted to assistant general. He participated in the Xiaozhan troop-training in 1895 and was appointed captain of engineer battalion, later promoted to garrison commander. He was transferred under an order to Beijing in 1902, in charge of guarding the end door of the Forbidden City. Thereafter, he was promoted to provincial commander-in-chief in Yunnan, Gansu and Jiangnan; grand coordinators of Jiangsu and Deputy Viceroy of Jiangxi and Jiangnan, later Nanyang Minister. After the Revolution of 1911, he was once appointed as the Military Governor of Jiangsu Province and the special envoy governing the Yangtze Area. However, he persisted in giving his allegiance to the Qing royalty and had his army men keep

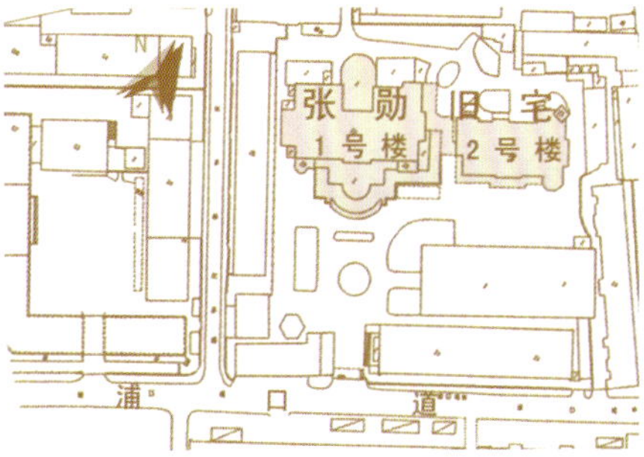

1号楼历史照片 Historic photo of No.1 Building

2号楼历史照片 Historic photo of No.2 Building

their Qing hairstyle, thus being named "Pigtail General". By making use of the "Controversy between Presidential Palace and State Council" between President Li Yuanhong and Secretary of State Duan Qirui, Zhang Xun led his army into Beijing in the name of "mediation" in 1917 and supported Puyi to restore his power, titled himself Grand Councilor, Viceroy of Zhili and Beiyang Minister. He lived in Tianjin after the defeat and was appointed superintendent for forestry and land reclamation in Rehe, but didn't take the office. He invested in banking business in Tianjin and constructed many buildings.

Built in early 1900s, the resident, designed by Germany architect Cort and Ruth Kigel, consisted of two separate brick-wood building, both being two-storied with red-tiled sloping roofs and stucco finished walls. A range of open colonnade was used to join the two constructions. The design presents the resident with lightness and exquisiteness as well as the harmony between the colors.

1号楼正立面渲染图 Facade Rendering of No.1 Building

2号楼正立面渲染图 Facade rendering of No.2 Building

2号楼背立面渲染图 Back elevation rendering of No.2 Building

内庭院 Inner Courtyard

瓷砖花饰 Floral tiles

↓外景瓷砖 Patterned tiles under the outer-eaves

老家具 Old-fashion furniture

老家具 Old-fashion furniture

家具雕饰 Carvings on the furniture

家具雕饰 Carvings on the furniture

楼梯与穿衣镜 Staircase and the pier glass

# Leopold Building
# 利华大楼

利华大楼位于和平区解放北路116号，天津市文物保护单位，特殊保护等级历史风貌建筑，建于1939年，占地面积约2 100m²，建筑面积约6 200m²，法商永和营造公司工程师穆乐设计，由比利时籍犹太人李亚溥（1902—？）投资兴建，是一座办公兼住宅的公寓式大楼，也是天津最早的具有现代技术和功能的高层建筑之一。该建筑主楼十层，高43m，钢筋混凝土框架结构，主楼外墙面采用深棕色麻面砖贴面，色彩稳重大方。建筑内部设两部电梯，布局合理。建筑构图采用非对称式，外部造型错落有致，属典型的现代主义风格。

外景 Exterior view

Listed as the heritage site under city protection and the special protection historic architecture in Tianjin, the Leopold Building is located at 116 North Jiefang Road, Heping District. It covers an area of about 2,100 square meters, and a floor area of about 6,200 square meters.

Invested by Marcel LeVopold(1902-?), a Swiss Jewish, the Leopold Building was designed by Mr. P. Muller, architect from a French engineering company—Hunke & Muller. Being an apartment-styled block, the Leopold Building was constructed in 1939 and served both for business and resident. It is considered as one of the earliest tall buildings with multifunction and modern technique in Tianjin at that time.

The main section of the Leopold Building is ten-storied with 43meters high and in reinforced concrete structure. The walls were faced with black-brown pockmark tiles, looking more magnificent and elegant. Two elevators were adapted in the structure. It is classified as a modern nonsymmetrical design considering its sections being with different heights.

外檐局部 Partial outer-eaves

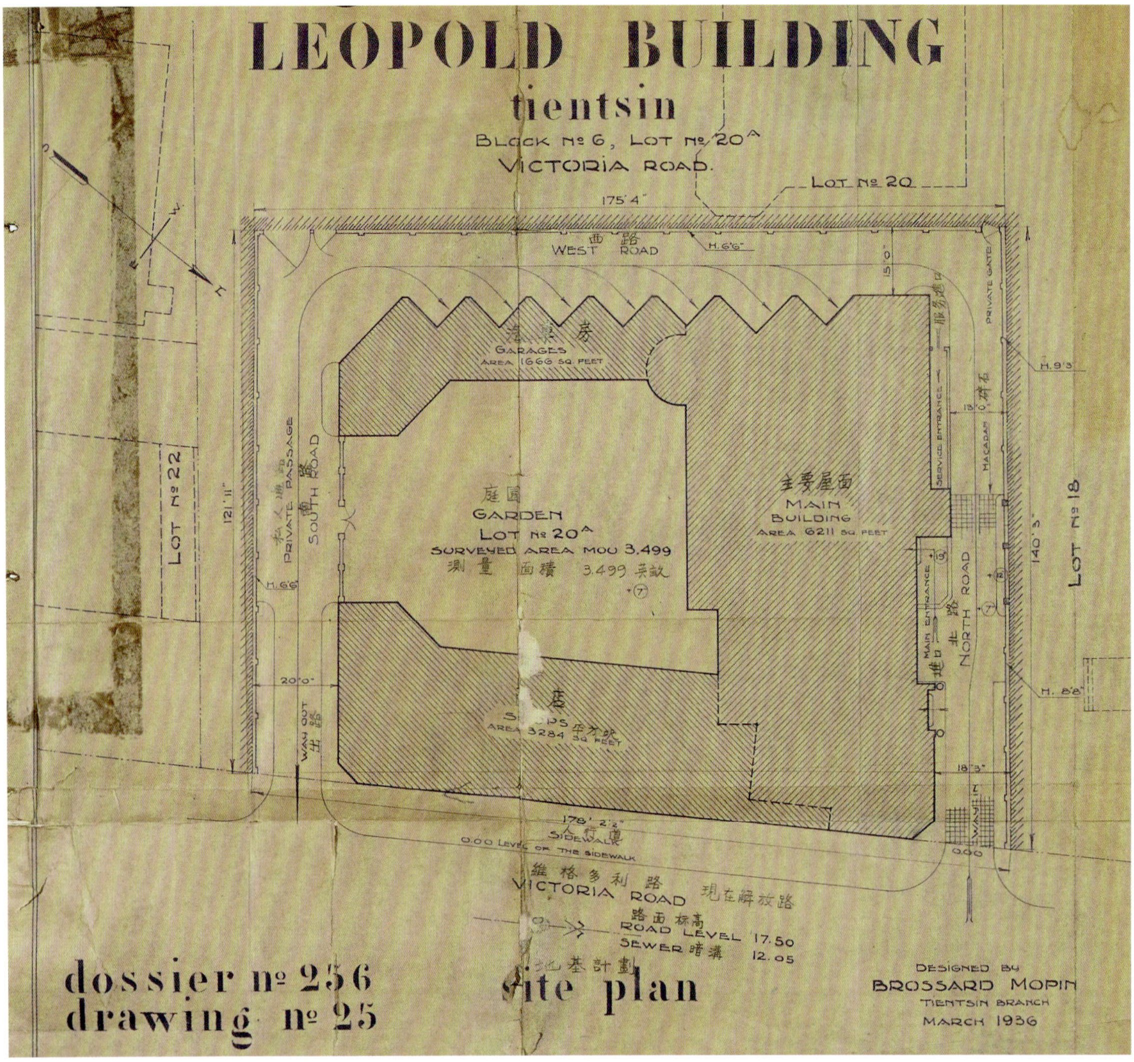


原设计图 Original blueprint

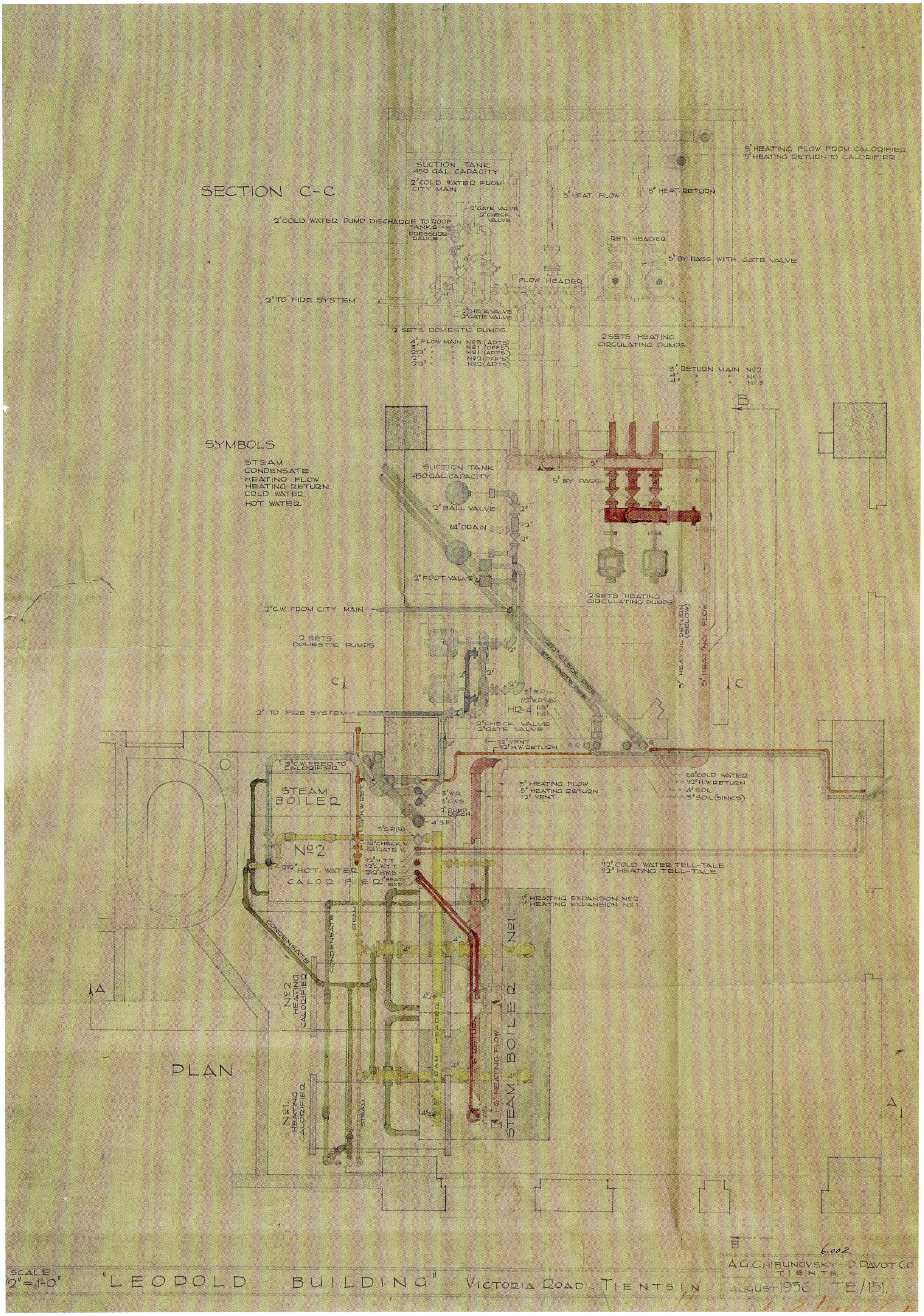
SECTION C-C.
SUCTION TANK 450 GAL. CAPACITY
2" COLD WATER FROM CITY MAIN
5" HEATING FLOW FROM CALORIFIER
5" HEATING RETURN TO CALORIFIER
5" HEAT FLOW
5" HEAT RETURN
RET. HEADER
5" BY PASS WITH GATE VALVE
FLOW HEADER
2" TO FIRE SYSTEM
2 SETS DOMESTIC PUMPS.
2 SETS HEATING CIRCULATING PUMPS.
SYMBOLS
STEAM
CONDENSATE
HEATING FLOW
HEATING RETURN
COLD WATER
HOT WATER
SUCTION TANK 450 GAL. CAPACITY
2" BALL VALVE
2" FOOT VALVE
2" C.W. FROM CITY MAIN
2 SETS DOMESTIC PUMPS
5" BY PASS
2 SETS HEATING CIRCULATING PUMPS
2" TO FIRE SYSTEM
2" CHECK VALVE
2" GATE VALVE
STEAM BOILER
Nº2
HOT WATER CALORIFIER
5" HEATING FLOW
5" HEATING RETURN
1/2" VENT
1/2" COLD WATER TELL-TALE
1/2" HEATING TELL-TALE
1" HEATING EXPANSION Nº2
1" HEATING EXPANSION Nº1
CONDENSATE
Nº2 HEATING CALORIFIER
Nº1 HEATING CALORIFIER
STEAM
STEAM BOILER Nº1
PLAN
SCALE: 1/2"=1'-0"
"LEOPOLD BUILDING" VICTORIA ROAD, TIENTSIN
A.G. CHIBUNOVSKY - P. PAVOT Co. TIENTSIN
AUGUST 1936 TE/151.

# Guangming Building
# 光明大楼

光明大楼位于和平区解放北路18~20号，重点保护等级历史风貌建筑，现为居住、商业用房。光明大楼也称“小雅克多利亚大楼”，建于二十世纪初，为公寓式住宅楼。该建筑占地面积约300 m$^2$，建筑面积约2 400 m$^2$，框架结构楼房，主体六层，局部七层。建筑平面以楼梯和电梯为中心组织居住单元。每个单元内暖气、卫生设施齐全。建筑外型既有现代建筑简洁挺拔的体量，又有部分西洋古典建筑的细部，具有折中主义建筑特征。

正立面渲染图 Facade Rendering

Located at 18~20 North Jiefang Road of Heping District, Guangming Building is an important protection historic architecture, and now residential and commercial. Built in early the 1900s as an apartment building, it has another name, Little Yakov Doria Building. It covers an area of 300 square meters and a floor area of 2,400 square meters. The building is a framed structure with six stories on the main building and seven stories partially. The staircases and lifts are the center to organize living units. Each living unit is equipped with heating and sanitary facilities. With the simplicity and magnificence of modern architecture and the characteristics of classic western architecture, the building is a typical eclectic architecture.

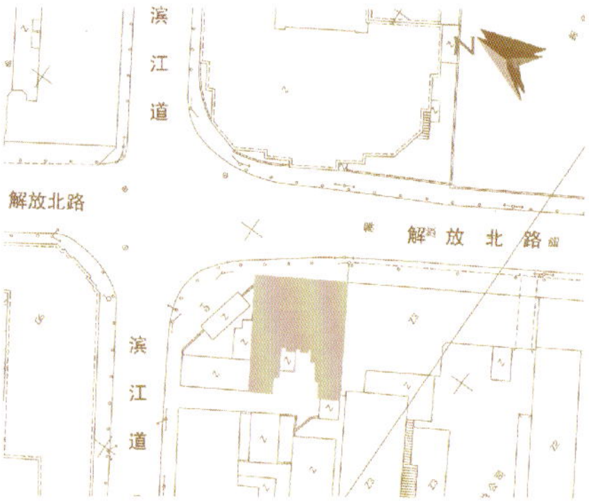


外檐局部 Partial outer-eaves

外檐窗 Window under the outer-eaves

外景 Exterior vie

# Huayuan Road Area
# 花园路地区

# Former Residence of Tian Zhongyu

# 田中玉旧宅

田中玉旧宅位于和平区营口道42号，天津市区、县文物保护单位，重点保护等级历史风貌建筑，现为办公用房。田中玉（1864—1935），字蕴山，河北抚宁人，皖系军阀，毕业于天津武备学堂。1907年他出任东三省督练公所总参议，辛亥革命后，历任代理山东民政长、曹州镇总兵、兖州镇守使、陆军次长、察哈尔都统，1919年任山东督军，并一度兼任省长。1923年山东发生土匪孙美瑶临城劫车案，被劫者包括外国旅客及记者等，劫案平息后，各国公使向北洋政府提出赔偿通牒，迫于压力，田中玉引咎辞职，寓居天津，投资纺织、金融及房地产。

该建筑建于1922年，占地面积约1 500 m$^2$，建筑面积约1 600 m$^2$，砖木结构三层楼房，设有地下室。建筑平面较规整，对称布局；外檐采用清水青砖墙面，红瓦坡顶；主入口用四根超大尺度的爱奥尼克巨柱支撑三角形山花，形成两层楼高的门厅，气势恢宏，显示了主人不甘寂寞、急欲表现的心情。

外景 Exterior view

Located at 42 Yingkou Avenue, Heping District, the Former Residence of Tian Zhongyu is the heritage site under city/county protection and the important protection historic architecture and is now an office building. Born in Funing, Hebei Province, Tian Zhongyu (1864–1935) had a courtesy name of Yunshan, a warlord of the Wan Xi. Graduating from Tianjin Military School, he was appointed chairman consultant of the office of military training in the three northeast provinces. After the Revolution of 1911, he was named deputy civil administer of Shandong Province, garrison commander of Caozhou Town, garrison commissioner of Yanzhou, vice chief of army and stadholder of Chahar. In 1919, he was appointed provincial military governor of Shandong Province and also governor for a time. In 1923, there happened the Train Hijacking by Bandit Sun Meiyao in Lincheng, Shandong Province, the hijacked included foreign tourists and journalists. After the hijacking was subsided, ministers from many countries proposed a diplomatic note of compensation to the Beiyang government. Tian Zhongyu resigned under pressure and moved to Tianjin and lived there, investing in textiles, finance and real estate.

The three-storied brick-timber building with basements was built in 1922, covering an area of about 1,500 square meters and a floor area of about 1,600 square meters. The building plane is relatively regular and symmetrically laid-out. The exterior wall is built by fair-faced black bricks. The roofs are red-tiled sloping ones. At the main entrance, four extremely large Ionic columns are used to support the triangular pediments, forming a hallway at the height of two stories with grand vigor, revealing the host's mood of unwilling to be lonely and being anxious to show off.

正立面渲染图 Facade Rendering

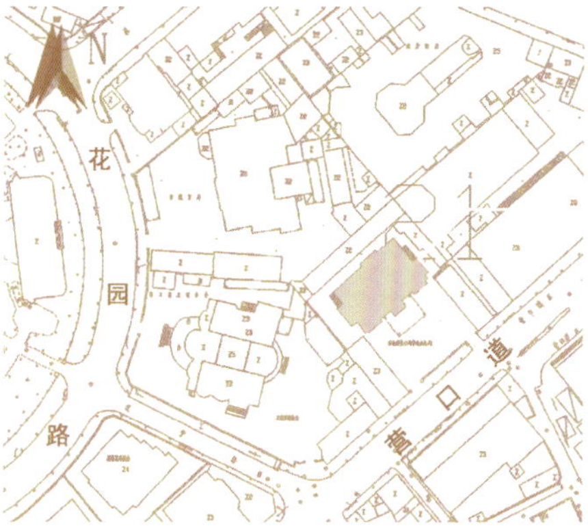


外檐局部 Partial outer-eaves

外檐花饰 Decorations under the outer-eaves

外景 Exterior view

壁炉 Fireplace

一楼门厅 Lobby on the first floor

木地板 Wooden floor

原设计图 Original blueprint

# Former Residence of Zhuang Lefeng

# 庄乐峰旧宅

庄乐峰旧宅位于和平区花园路10号，天津市文物保护单位，重点保护等级历史风貌建筑，现为办公用房。庄乐峰（1873—1949），名仁松，号乐峰，江苏丹阳人，毕业于天津北洋水师学堂，初任开平矿务局翻译，后参与筹办山东枣庄中兴煤矿，任该矿董事，并任美商胜家缝纫机公司买办。作为实业家，庄乐峰曾任天津英租界华人纳税会董事长多年。经他提议，从1927年开始，提取英租界华人纳税款的18%，创办了租界内第一所华人学校——天津公学，后改名为耀华学校。

该建筑建于1926年，占地面积约2 700 m$^2$，建筑面积约3 500 m$^2$，由德国建筑师毕伦特设计。建筑为混合结构三层楼房，设有地下室。建筑造型以古典复兴为主，但依据地形布局，不强调对称；建筑主入口及正立面设简化的罗马柱廊，柱间栏杆均有镂空花饰；屋顶采用法国孟莎式；外檐墙面以混水墙和清水红砖墙搭配，和谐而又温馨；室内装修豪华考究，保存良好。

右侧立面渲染图 Rendering of the right-side elevation

精美的石雕 Exquisite stone-carvings

Located at 10 Huayuan Road, Heping District, the Former Residence of Zhuang Lefeng is the heritage site under city protection and the important protection historic architecture and is now an office building. Zhuang Lefeng (1873–1949), named Rensong and a sobriquet of Lefeng, was born in Danyang, Jiangsu Province. Graduating from the Beiyang Naval College in Tianjin, he first worked as a translator in Kaiping Mining Administration and later participated in the establishment of Zhongxing Mine in Zaozhuang, Shangdong Province, being a director in the mine and a comprador for American Singer Sewing Machine Co., Ltd. As an industrialist, he took the post of the chairman on board of the General Meeting of Tax Payers in the British concession in Tianjin for many years. Under his proposals, 18% of the tax paid by the Chinese in the British

concession was withdrawn from the year 1927 to build the first Chinese school in concessions—Tianjin College, later named Yaohua School. Designed by a German architect named Berent, the building was constructed in 1926, covering an area of about 2,700 square meters with a floor area of about 3,500 square meters. The three-storied mixed structured building had basements. The architectural modeling focused on classical revival, but composed on the basis of landform, without emphasizing symmetry. Simplified Roman colonnade were located at the main entrance and the front facade; handrails among columns were decorated with hollow-out carvings; a French style Mansard roof was adopted; exterior walls were built with furred wall and dry wall by red bricks, harmonious and warm; interior finish was luxury and carefully selected, all under sound preservation.

楼梯间 Staircase

共享大厅 Sharing hall

外景 Exterior view

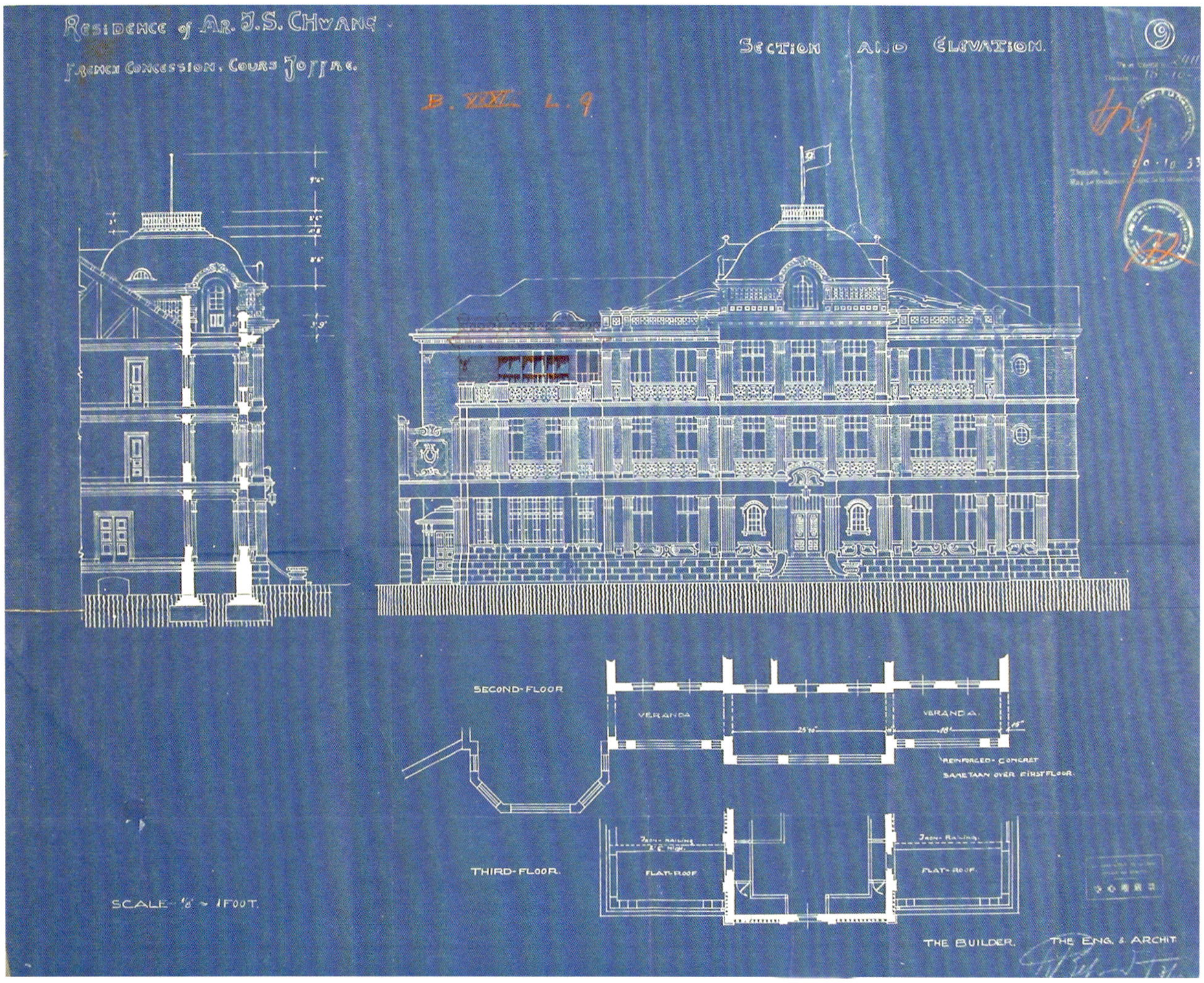

原设计图 Original blueprint

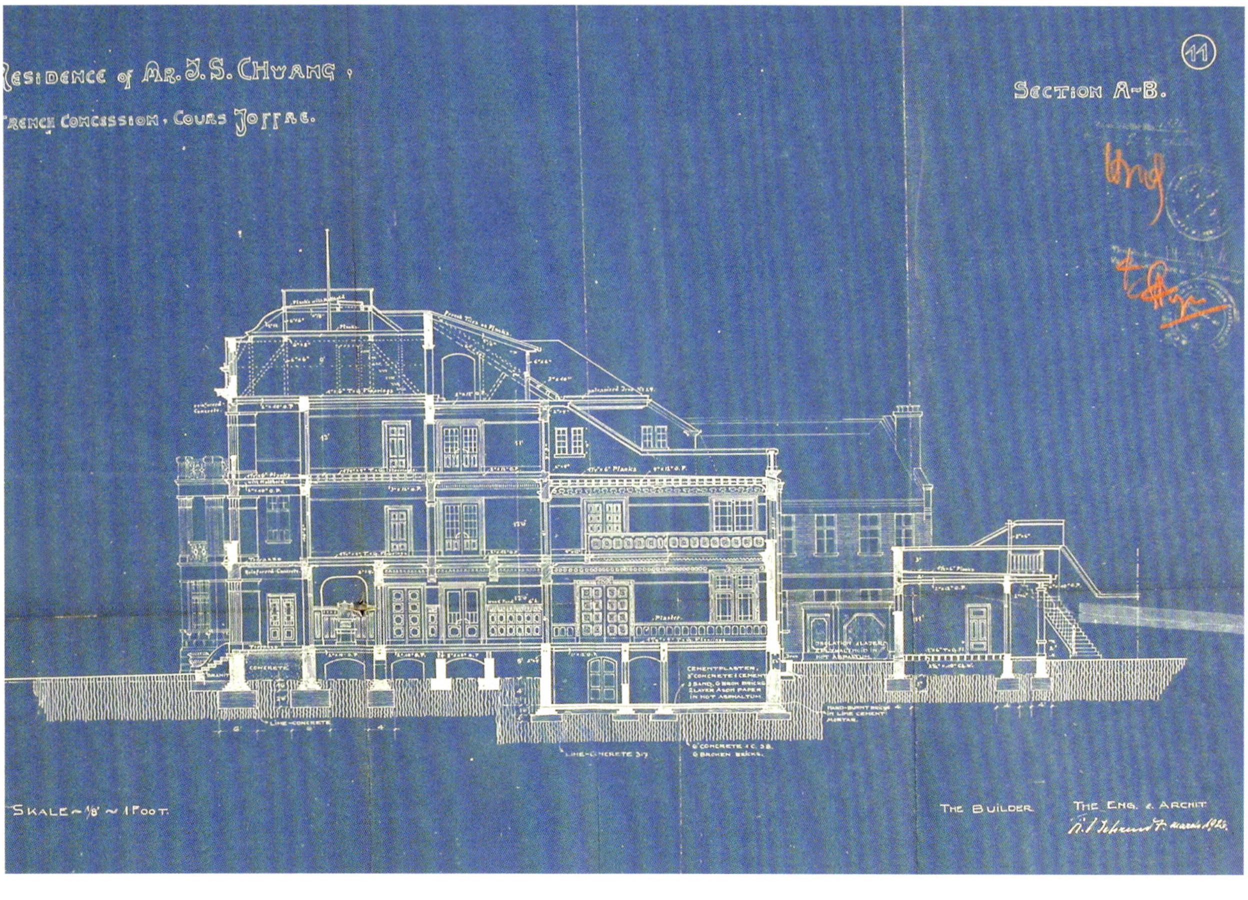

内檐门 Gate under the inner-eaves

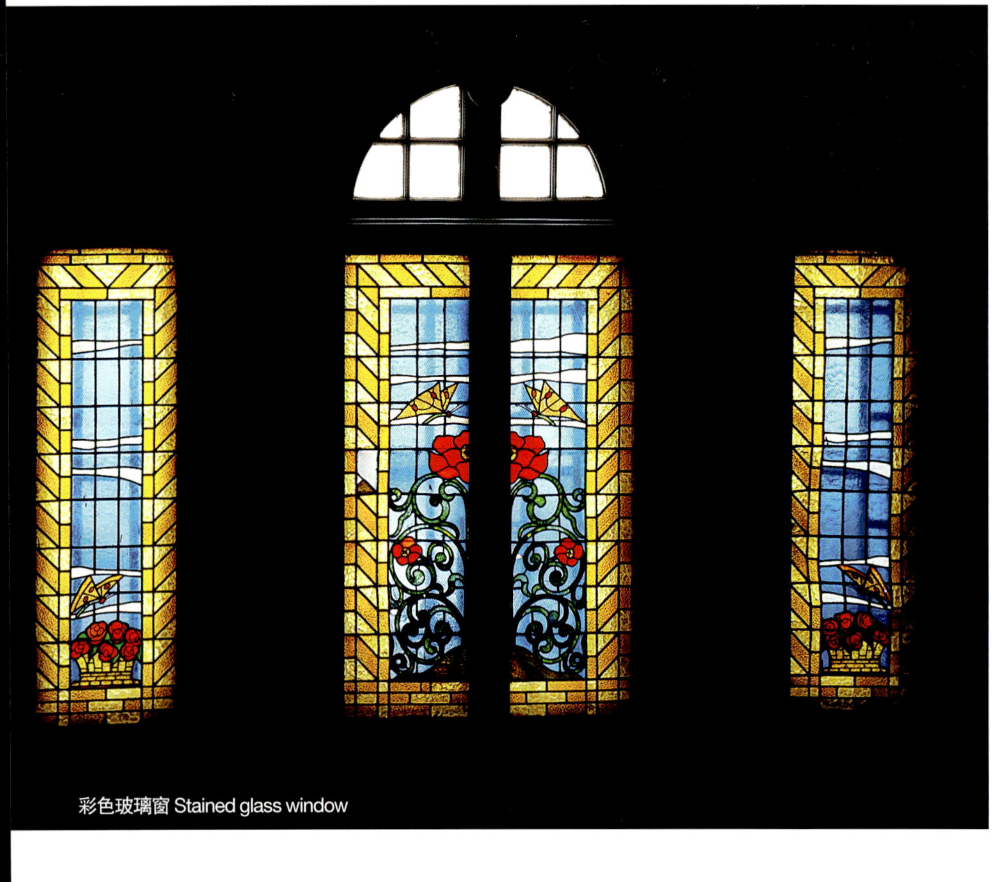

彩色玻璃窗 Stained glass window

# Former Residence of Li Jifu

# 李吉甫旧宅

李吉甫旧宅位于和平区花园路12号，天津市文物保护单位，特殊保护等级历史风貌建筑，现为办公用房。李吉甫（？—1927），天津人，英商仁记洋行买办。李氏家族是天津本帮（北帮）买办的典型代表，世称“仁记李”。“仁记李”第一代李辅臣（？—1910），曾在天津仁记洋行当佣工，因识别白银成色且善经营，被提升为会计司事，1895年升任该行帮办、买办。为方便农畜产品出口，仁记在全国各地设有仓库，就地加工羊毛、驼绒、皮张，以及猪鬃、马尾、棉花、青麻、桃仁、杏仁、草帽辫等，几至包揽了原产地的收购，以此称雄天津出口市场。李辅臣死后，仁记买办一职由其子李吉甫充任，李吉甫死后由其弟李志年接办。父子相继三十余年，积累大量财富，曾投资房地产，在英、法租界广置楼房和豪宅。

该建筑建于1918年，占地面积约5 400 m$^2$，建筑面积约4 400 m$^2$，由乐利工程司瑞士建筑师陆甫设计，砖木结构二层楼房（设有地下室），是中式四合院布局的西洋建筑楼群，有两组由回廊相连的楼房构成，回廊由二十根塔什干式柱支撑。建筑造型对称稳重，立面变化丰富，室内外细部以古典雕饰为主，造型各异。

鸟瞰图 Bird' s eye view

正立面渲染图 Facade Rendering

The Former Residence of Li Jifu is located at 12 Huayuan Road, Heping District, listed as the heritage site under city protection and the important protection historic architecture in Tianjin and is a office building nowadays. Born in Tianjin, Li Jifu (?–1927) served as a comprador for the Gibb Livingston & Co., a British business. Li's Family was a typical representative of local Tianjin (Northern Faction) compradors, popularly named "Renji Li". The first generation of "Renji Li" was Li Fuchen (?–1910), who had worked in Gibb Livingston & Co., (Tianjin). Thanks for the capacity of identifying the fineness of silver and good management, he was promoted to chief accountant and then assistant-in-managing as well as comprador for the company after 1895. To facilitate the export of agricultural and animal products, he set up branches and warehouses in many places across the country and processed wool, camel wool, animal skins, hog bristle, horsetail, cotton, abutilon, peach seeds, almonds and straw plaits etc. He even monopolized the purchase in the origin, thus making him renowned in Tianjin export market. After the death of Li Fuchen, comprador of Gibb Livingston & Co., was succeeded by his son Li Jifu, and then Li Zhinian after the death of Li Jifu, his younger brother. The father and sons took the position for over 30 years and accumulated large fortune. They invested in real estates, buying many buildings and luxurious houses in the British and French concessions.

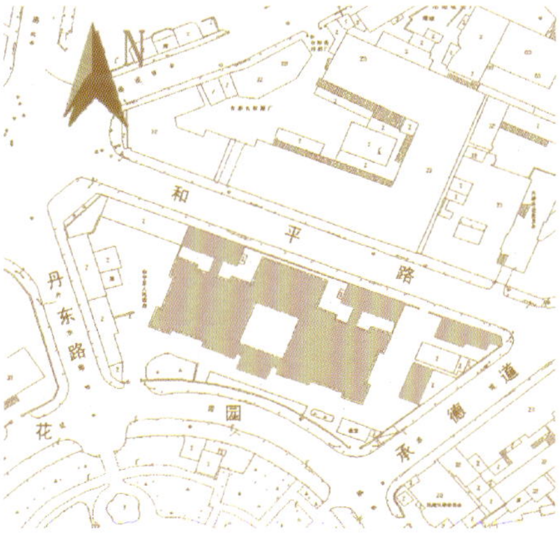

Designed by Loup, a Swiss architect, the building was built in 1918, covering an area of about 5,400 square meters and its floor area was about 2,100 square meters. The brick-wood architecture is two-storied with the basement. The residence is made up of two western building complexes, but arranged a Chinese traditional courtyard. The two complexes are joined with a cloister formed by 20 columns of the Tuscan order. The architecture is a symmetrical design, tasting more massive and steady. Rich in variation of the elevations, classical carvings of sorts are adopted to decorate the details both inside and outside.

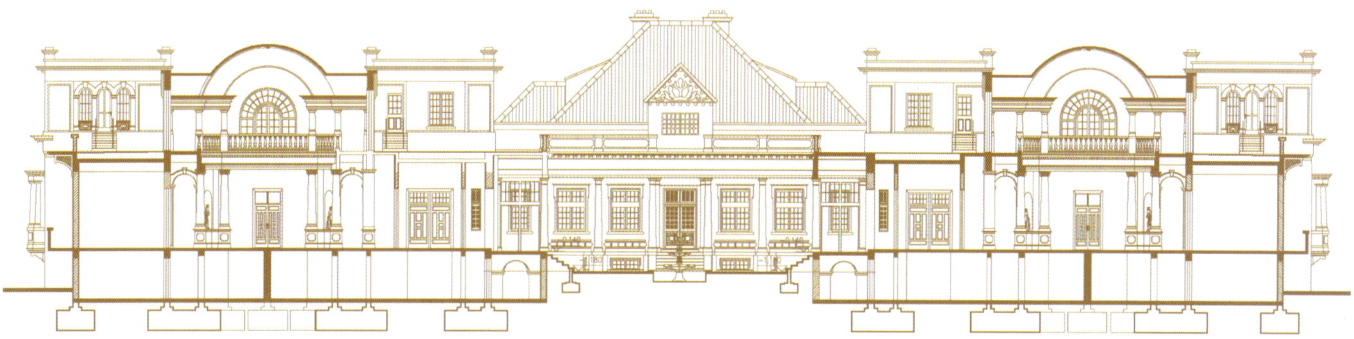

外景 Exterior view

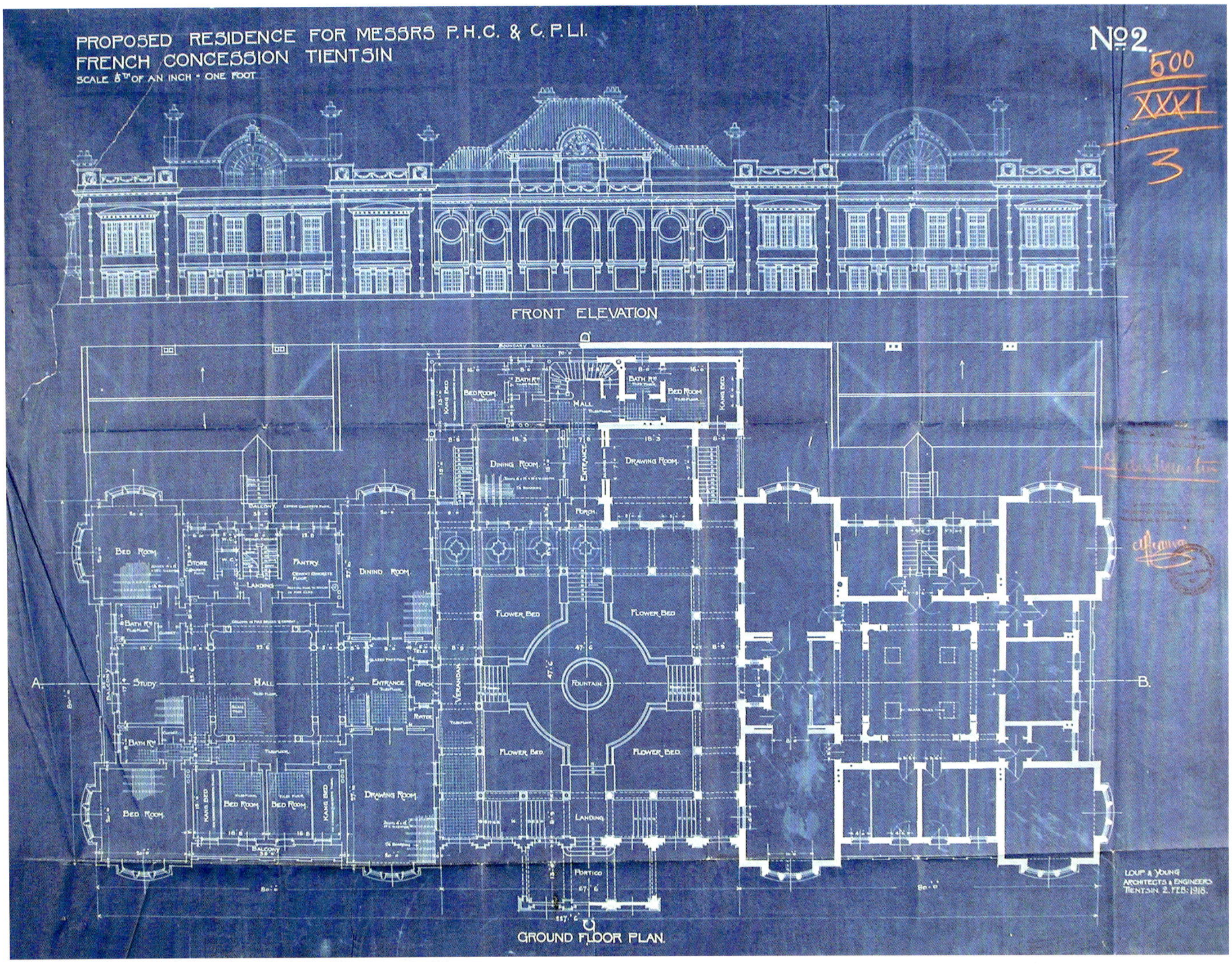

原设计图 Original blueprint

外景 Exterior view

庭院 Garden

内景 Inner view

内檐局部
Partial under the inner-eaves

楼梯 Stairs

# Former Residence of Zhang Ruiting

# 章瑞庭旧宅

章瑞庭旧宅位于和平区花园路9号，天津市文物保护单位，重点保护等级历史风貌建筑，现为天津市工商业联合会。章瑞庭（1878—1944），天津人，著名实业家。因得小站练兵军官资助，他开办了恒记德军衣庄，专为小站供应军需，继而为各派系军阀承办军衣，如东北军服装即全由恒记德承做。章瑞庭后以雄厚的资金，开办恒源帆布工厂、恒源纺织股份有限公司，并接办北洋纱厂。他曾资助南开学校教育基金十万元，该校礼堂特命名为瑞庭礼堂。

该建筑建于1922年，占地面积约2 500m$^2$，建筑面积约2 300m$^2$，由奥地利建筑师盖苓设计，砖木结构三层楼房（设有地下室和阁楼），混水墙面。首层前廊入口处为半圆形花厅，上设透明玻璃顶，玻璃窗采用彩色玻璃拼镶成风景图画，厅内设喷水池，设施豪华；屋顶为红色孟莎式，造型独特，外形虚实对比；外檐的古典柱式和宝瓶栏杆精美得当，具有古典主义建筑特征。

正立面渲染图 Facade Rendering

外景 Exterior view

The Former Residence of Zhang Ruiting was built at 9 Huayuan Road, Heping District, listed as the heritage site under city protection and the important protection historic architecture in Tianjin and now is Tianjin Federation of Industry and Commerce. Born in Tianjin and being a quite famous industrialist, Zhang Ruiting(1878–1944) was well known as the founder of several enterprises one after another. Due to the funding by the officers of training troops in Xiaozhan, he founded Hengjide Military Uniform Store to provide military supplies for Xiaozhan troops, and then the store was assigned to provide military uniforms for each cliques, for instance, the uniforms of Northeast Army were all made by Hengjide. Afterwards, he set up Hengyuan Canvas Plant and Hengyuan Textile Co., Ltd. with abundant funds. Beiyang Cotton Mill was even taken over by him. He had subsidized 100,000 Yuan educational fund to Naikai School, the auditorium of which was named after him.

Designed by Austrian architect Rolf Geyling, the building was built in 1922. With the stucco finished walls, basement and attic, the brick-wood building is three-storied, and it covers an area of about 2,500 square meters and its floor area was about 2,300 square meters. A glass roofed structure in shape of a semicircle serves as the Entrance Hall (known as the floral hall), tasting luxurious because of its elegant decorations and the fountain inside as well as its stained glass windows. The Mansard roofs and columniation combined with balusters at the outer-eaves provide the architecture with a typically classical atmosphere.

原设计图 Original blueprint

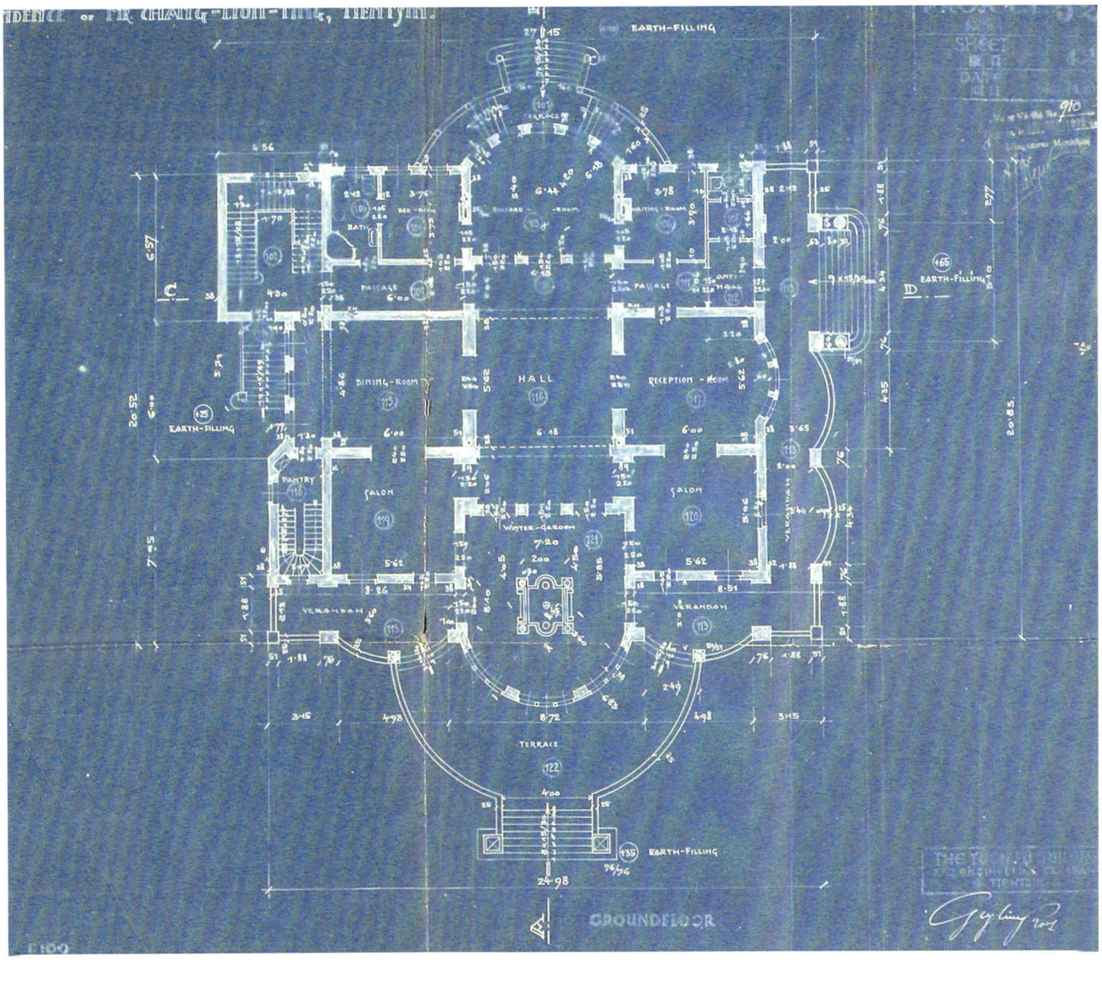

内景 Inner view

彩色玻璃窗 Stained glass window

彩色玻璃窗 Stained glass window

老瓷砖 Old-fashioned tiles

木雕细部 Detailed wood carving

图书在版编目（CIP）数据

居住建筑.1/路红主编. －天津：天津大学出版社，2010.5
（天津历史风貌建筑）
ISBN 978－7－5618－3471－8
Ⅰ.①居… Ⅱ.①路… Ⅲ.①名人－故居－简介－天津市②名人－生平事迹－天津市 Ⅳ.①K878.2②K820.821
中国版本图书馆CTP数据核字(2010)第071288号

组稿编辑 韩振平
责任编辑 韩振平

出版发行 天津大学出版社
地　　址 天津市卫津路92号天津大学内(邮编:300072)
电　　话 发行部:022-27403647　邮购部:022-27402742
网　　址 publish.tju.edu.cn
印　　刷 北京华联印刷有限公司
经　　销 全国各地新华书店
开　　本 210mm×285mm
印　　张 18
字　　数 260千
版　　次 2010年5月第1版
印　　次 2022年1月第1版第2次印刷
定　　价 178.00元